CREATIVE CAMPING

Joy Mackay

a division of SP Publications, Inc.
WHEATON, ILLINOIS 60187

Offices also in
Whitby, Ontario, Canada
Amersham-on-the-Hill, Bucks, England

Most of the Scripture quotations in this book are from the *New International Version,* © 1978 by the New York International Bible Society. Other quotations are from *The Living Bible* (TLB), © 1971 by Tyndale House; the *New American Standard Bible* (NASB), © 1960, 1962, 1963, 1968, 1971, 1972, 1973, 1975, 1977 by the Lockman Foundation; and *The New Testament in Modern English* by J.B. Phillips (PH), © 1958, The Macmillan Company. Used by permission.

Cover photo courtesy of Honey Rock Camp, Eagle River, Wisconsin.

Recommended Dewey Decimal Classification: 796.5422
Suggested Subject Heading: CAMPING

Library of Congress Catalog Card Number: 83-051301
ISBN: 0-88207-621-3

Originally published in 1966 as *Creative Counseling for Christian Camps*/ published in 1977 as *Creative Camping*

Printed in the United States of America

VICTOR BOOKS
A divison of SP Publications, Inc.
Wheaton, Illinois 60187

Contents

Publisher's Foreword

For several years we've been asking evangelical camp leaders, "What kind of Christian camp publication do you need most?"

Nearly unanimously they reply, "A more comprehensive book on counselor training." Some add that the average Christian camp's program takes little advantage of camp's major distinctive: God's great outdoors. Such a camp could convene indoors all summer (given a large gym and a swimming pool), without having to curtail many activities.

But there is an encouraging trend. Each year an increasing number of Christian camp directors are giving their programs an outdoor flavor. Realizing that kids crave adventure, they're specializing in activities that young people can't engage in back home.

Each summer author Joy Mackay teaches at the Summer Institute of Camping, Schroon Lake, New York. During the rest of the year she teaches camping and other education subjects at Central State University, Wilberforce, Ohio. Like other top leaders in the camping field, she believes in training counselors in outdoor living and camping skills they can pass on to their campers. This open-sky type of camping calls for counselors who are more than mere baby-sitters or chaperones. It doesn't work with counselors who can't cope with thunderstorms and bugs.

Since most Christian camps are already strong on Bible-teaching and evangelism, author Mackay didn't make these the major emphases of this book. But there are helpful tips for Bible hours, campfire meetings, campers' quiet times, cabin devotions, memorizing Scripture, leading campers to Christ, and teaching missions.

If your camp is typical, you don't use the outdoors as much as the author suggests. When you come to an outdoor idea you haven't used, why not try it—before camp? If you're young at heart (all counselors should be), you'll find it fun to swing an ax, paddle a canoe, hit a target, navigate by map and compass, lay special kinds of fires, or scuba dive. If you learn a new skill or two, it will help you get closer to some campers, which in turn will aid you in helping them know your Lord better.

Counselors can be more creative campers. It's our prayer that this revised and expanded edition of *Creative Camping* will help thousands of counselors in winning and training campers for Christ.

Me! A Counselor!

So you are going to be a camp counselor! If this summer will be your first time, you might picture yourself living in a cabin in the woods by a lake, surrounded by tall pine trees. You'll swim, water ski, hike, go boating, get plenty of sunshine. Sounds glamorous.

But camping won't be all vacation. It may be the hardest work you have ever done, but it can also be the most satisfying and rewarding summer you have ever had.

Christian camping is growing fast today. Evangelical leaders are realizing the many opportunities at camp to impart spiritual truths. So more and more churches, groups of churches, denominations, and individuals are using this effective tool of Christian education. More and more churches are rounding out their total church programs with a few weeks of summer camp.

Perhaps you have heard the claim that often more is accomplished in a young person's life during a week of camp than in a whole year of Sunday School or church. Why is this claim made? Because camp has a concentrated impact on campers. They do not leave after campfire to stop at McDonald's, or to go home to watch TV.

Camp provides many consecutive hours of Christian influence with few distractions. If a young person attends Sunday School, morning and evening church services, and youth meetings, his church is contacting him only 5 or 6 hours a week, and these are not all at one time. A church-related camp offers a 24-hour controlled Christian environment, a climate of freedom for the Holy Spirit to work, and hourly demonstrations of Christian living through the staff's example. A good Christian camp is not only a strong arm of evangelism for the local church but a laboratory for testing Christian living.

A well-trained counselor helps his Christian camp make a great impact on youth. For the quality of the counseling staff is much more important than the site, the facilities, and the program put together.

Counseling is a privilege. If you know Christ's transforming power in your own life, you may be privileged to be His channel to others in one of the most fruitful areas of Christian service—camp.

The Lord has told us to be His witnesses "in all Judea and Samaria, and to the ends of the earth" (Acts 1:8). Camp this summer may be your Judea or Samaria.

Why Do Counselors Need Training?

If you believe that the Lord's work is important you will want to do it in the best way possible. If you believe that personal decisions for Christ are essential and that good habits of Christian living such as prayer, Bible study, personal devotions, and witnessing should be established, you will not want to leave these to chance. You will want to get all the help you can in these areas.

Good camps put much emphasis on staff training. Their leaders recognize the importance of training in order to effectively help campers adjust socially and develop good characters. In a Christian camp we strive to do this and more. A Christian camp provides an atmosphere where the Holy Spirit can work through dedicated counselors to change campers' lives.

How Will Counselor Training Help You?

1. Counselor training will make you more confident in your job. Probably you are more willing to undertake a job when you feel well prepared for it, and know what is expected of you.
2. You will become more health- and safety-conscious. Camp will be a safer, healthier place for you and your campers.
3. You will feel more at home in God's great outdoors.
4. Because of training, your ministry as a counselor will be more effective and your campers will benefit more from their stay at camp.
5. Because camp enjoys a good public image, many non-Christian parents send their children to Christian camps where they know counselors really care. You will have opportunities to reach campers for Christ that pastors or professional Christian workers will not have.
6. If you are a Sunday School teacher, a summer camp experience will give you new insights and understandings that will carry over into your teaching.
7. If you are a youth worker or club leader, you will profit by getting closer to your boys or girls. You will see them in informal situations and they will get to know you as a leader, friend, and confidant.
8. If you are a pastor, camping will give you better rapport with young people and new approaches to their problems.
9. If you are a college student, you will learn new skills in human relations. (Many a student has found God's will for his own life while counseling with young people.)
10. If you are a parent, counseling will broaden your understanding of today's youth.
11. Whatever your station in life, counselor training and camp counseling should help you grow as a person into a more mature, integrated, well-balanced Christian.

Are you willing to be God's channel this summer? If you are, look forward expectantly to what He will do through you!

1 Being a Counselor

Camp exists for the camper, yet it can be one of the greatest experiences of a counselor's life. It can broaden your vision, open new doors of service, give you insights into working with people, and contribute to your own spiritual growth and maturity in Christ. Though your own growth is not the primary function of camp, it is an important by-product of a good camp.

No matter what your background—college student, housewife, businessman, or pastor—the Holy Spirit wants to use you to accomplish His purposes in the lives of your campers.

If this is your first experience in camp, you may be keenly aware of how your new situation contrasts with the business world. Instead of a "What can I get out of this?" attitude, camp counselors need to ask, "How much can I give of myself?"

Demands on Counselors

You need to be living victoriously in Christ in order to help campers with their problems. If you are on top of your own problems, you can be free to minister to campers (Mark 10:45).

You must like children and enjoy their company while being their counselor. You must be able to tolerate long contacts with campers, for counseling is hard work. You have a 24-hour-a-day responsibility for your campers. Many times you are tired physically. You need to discipline your time and your hours of sleep, to enable you to be physically fit to give your best for God each day.

You need to jealously guard your time alone with the Lord each day. Many legitimate duties can easily crowd out this important time. But no number of services or Bible messages can take the place of your own quiet time. You need a daily infilling from the Lord, so that the life of Christ may flow out through you to your campers.

Constant demands will be made on you. The time you had set aside for writing a letter may be the time when Joe wants to talk with you. So you set aside the unfinished letter to engage Joe in conversation, because God has trusted you with this 12-year-old boy for the week. You are showing Joe by example that God has time for him too.

You may be called on to improvise, to substitute in an activity, or to try something entirely new to you because of some emergency. There may be sacrifices of your time, of self, of personal pleasure. But the rewards far exceed the sacrifice. To see the glow on Jan's face after a campfire meeting, to see the change in Jim's life, are worth it all a hundred times. "For even the Son of man did not come to be served, but to serve, and to give" (Mark 10:45). This verse may come back to you often as you minister for Him.

As a counselor, you must demonstrate emotional maturity. You assume responsibility for your own actions without making excuses. You need to adjust easily to changes in your schedule and be able to take disappointments in stride. You had planned to take Tuesday off for a picnic and double date with other staff members when your day off was changed. How you react may be a better indication of your maturity than your glowing testimony around the campfire. A mature and well-integrated person feels good about himself and others. Check your own maturity with this self-evaluation. Can you realistically evaluate your strengths and weaknesses?

My Strengths and Weaknesses

	Below Average *(Need to improve in this area)*	Average *(Can be developed more)*	Above Average *(Must use these qualities)*
Emotional Maturity			
I accept criticism without being hurt or overly sensitive.			
I am tolerant of others' faults.			
I refrain from repeating gossip.			
I put the happiness and welfare of others above my own.			
I face problems objectively and do not make excuses.			
I get along well with people.			
I am loyal to friends and those for whom I work.			
I can make sound decisions fairly quickly and abide by these decisions.			
I have the courage of my convictions, regardless of popularity.			
I can control my temper.			
I work democratically with others. I am not authoritarian in leading them.			
I do not ask for special favors.			
I am not overly touchy or temperamental. I am prompt and businesslike in keeping records.			
I am dependable.			
Social Maturity			
I am a cheerful person.			
I am tactful—do not usually offend others.			
I possess a sense of humor, even when the joke is on me.			
I use good English when I speak.			
I consider myself poised in most situations.			

	Below Average *(Need to improve in this area)*	Average *(Can be developed more)*	Above Average *(Must use these qualities)*
Social Maturity (continued)			
I enjoy hard work.			
I have many varied interests.			
I am an enthusiastic person and am outgoing toward others.			
I am neat in my appearance.			
My clothing and I are kept clean.			
I like children and enjoy their company.			
I can teach or assist in several camp skills.			
I am able to work well as a member of a group.			
I assume responsibility and am conscientious in performing my duties.			
I am familiar with the out-of-doors.			
I am completely honest with myself and with others.			
I keep campers' confidences and share them with no one, not even to have others "pray about it."			
I can see a job to be done and do it without being told.			
I adapt easily to new situations.			
Health			
I know my own limitations and can live within them.			
I discipline myself in eating, hours of sleep, and use of time.			
I possess good health and vitality.			
I can participate in a vigorous activity program.			
I have recently had a physical examination. (Most camps require this of campers and staff before camp.)			

	Below Average *(Need to improve in this area)*	Average *(Can be developed more)*	Above Average *(Must use these qualities)*
Spiritual Maturity			
I know Jesus Christ as my personal Lord and Saviour and enjoy a vital and growing relationship with Him.			
Working with the Holy Spirit, I can lead a camper to Christ using language and terms the camper understands.			
My life is a good example, the kind I want campers to follow.			
I have a regular time of fellowship with my Lord in the Word and in prayer each day.			
I am concerned that each of my campers grows in his spiritual life during his stay in my cabin.			
I am able to relate the Word of God to my campers' everyday lives.			

Filling Out Your Application

Your first contact with camp may be a letter in which you request an application form (see sample staff application, p. 201). Some camps use a very simple form; others have many pages to fill out. Some ask for a brief biography of your life, a transcript of your grades (if you are in school), and a picture of yourself. You may even be asked to solve typical campers' problems.

Whatever the form, take time to fill it out carefully, especially if you have not counseled previously at the camp. Type, print, or write neatly.

Evaluate yourself objectively. Don't try to oversell yourself or you may not be able to live up to your director's expectations. But don't undersell your abilities either. Your director is interested in knowing about any previous camping or leadership experience you have had. If you taught a Sunday School class or helped in Vacation Bible School, say so. The director also wants to know your educational qualifications. (Include any courses in camping or related subjects.) List the areas of camp where you feel qualified to make a contribution. Give him the information clearly and concisely.

If references are called for, an employer or college professor might be in a position to evaluate your industry or work performance. Your pastor can provide information on your faithfulness in church attendance and your leadership ability. Be sure to secure permission to use the names of your references *before* using them.

If a personal interview is requested, be punctual, neatly dressed, and honest and frank in answering questions. This is also an opportunity for you to ask questions about the camp and its policies. Find out the date when you are expected to be at camp and the date you may leave. Some camps run all summer and may conflict with your university or college calendar. Remember, if you commit yourself to stay until Labor Day, you must stay even if school starts the next day. You will want to ask about the camp's philosophy, remuneration, if any, and job descriptions (see Appendix, pp. 201-206). Let the director know what contribution you expect to make to the camp. Ask questions before you sign a contract, for your signature means you are committed to that camp. Do not cancel if you get a better offer later on.

For a good working relationship, you should feel sure that this is the Lord's place of service for you this summer. And the camp director also should be fairly sure that the Lord wants you to work at his camp.

Knowing Your God-given Responsibilities

To your director:
You are responsible for your job of counseling. This means you are to live up to the responsibilities outlined in your job analysis. You are to be prompt at all meetings and in complet-

ing reports. You are to observe all camp regulations cheerfully and encourage others to do the same.

Keep the welfare of your campers uppermost and the objectives of your camp always in mind. Show a friendly, cooperative spirit and demonstrate enthusiasm. Ask for no special favors or considerations. Be a good advertisement for your camp—and for your Lord.

To other staff members:

Be friendly, helpful, and loyal to each co-worker. Though some are quite different in personality from you, show appreciation for everyone's contribution. To help insure that camp will be an enriching experience for you, refrain from unfavorable discussions of personalities and from complaining. Demonstrate oneness and unity in Christ. "All men [and all campers] will know that you are My disciples if you love one another" (John 13:35).

You will need to work cooperatively with all staff members. Both counselors and operational staff must work together as a team. Cooks and maintenance people often work long hours and do not always see the life changes that counselors see. Sharing with them answers to prayer and results of their ministry can be encouraging. Good camp morale and congenial working relationships are essential. You must be able to show empathy not only toward your campers but to the rest of the staff as well.

Avoid cliques; be friendly to everyone. Avoid competing with other leaders for popularity among the campers. Often the most popular counselor does not have the most lasting influence on campers. Sometimes it's the quiet, conscientious staff member, who spends time with each of his campers, who is remembered long after camp ends.

To parents:

You may be asked to keep in touch with your campers' parents by letter or card each week. If so, assure them that Paul is being well cared for. Tell them when Mary passed her swimming test or when Tommy completed his project in the craft shop.

Many parents have fears when they send a child to camp for the first time. They want to know that their child is well, enjoying himself, happy, making friends, eating well, and having a good time. Christian parents are concerned also about their child's spiritual progress. Your reassurance will mean much to parents.

Consult your unit leader or director before writing about a camper's problems. A parent questionnaire (see p. 206) may aid you in writing parents and may help you understand why parents sent their son or daughter to camp.

To campers:
They are your responsibility for a week or more. They are looking for a friend. They want a counselor who will help them grow, become independent, and make wise decisions. They want a counselor who will enjoy camp experiences with them. They are looking to see if Christianity works—if it is demonstrated in your life—if what you say agrees with what you are. They want a counselor who is friendly without partiality. They want firmness with love, for this is security. They want to be noticed, to belong, not to get lost in the shuffle of a large crowd. Your campers want someone to understand them, to listen to them, to give encouragement for a job well done. They watch your every move. Nothing you do will go unnoticed. You are teaching continuously by your attitude and example.

Do you want your habits, your mannerisms, your dress to be copied by campers? Many campers are hero-worshipers. You will see yourself reflected in them in the least expected ways, not only in a skit on stunt night when they portray a day in your cabin. Show them a zest for life. Demonstrate to campers the abundant Christian life they hear about, but may have never seen. Share with them your love for the out-of-doors, and a youthful spirit regardless of the number of candles on your birthday cake! Besides a fun-loving personality, campers want a counselor who can teach some new skill. Can you build a fire in the rain? Can you paddle a canoe in white water? Can you find your way in the woods?

Serving Your Saviour

At camp you lead a varied existence. You are mother, dad, instructor, friend, and pal, all at the same time. You set the pace for the camp period. You try to guide your campers' energies along constructive lines. You try to be alert and sensitive to Penny's individual needs, realizing that all of camp is a learning experience.

You are alert to the health and safety of your campers. Watch for signs of fatigue, often shown by irritability. Perhaps Jane needs extra sleep, or Peter needs to be pulled out of swim class for an extra rest hour. Be alert for possible preludes to childhood diseases or colds such as sore throats, watery eyes, and runny noses. Observe your campers for bites, scratches, or cuts. Send or take casualties to the camp nurse. A few moments of precaution may avert a serious illness or prevent the spread of germs.

Is all this part of counseling? Ready to quit before you start? Evaluate your God-given abilities honestly. Then recall Paul's words: "I can do everything God asks me to with the help of Christ who gives me the strength and power" (Phil. 4:13, TLB).

Know Your After-camp Responsibilities

Records:

Last year's camper records, if your camp had them, were valuable to understanding your campers this year. (If your camp didn't keep such records, you probably wish that they had.)

Before you leave camp, record some information on each of your campers. Perhaps you will use a camper evaluation form like the one on page 205. You will be recording the skills that Bill developed during camp, the swimming test he passed, his interests, his stronger and weaker qualities, his spiritual decision, the apparent results of your personal counseling with him, etc.

Some camps have their counselors make three copies of the camper evaluation form. They send one copy each to Bill's pastor and Sunday School teacher, if he attends church. This helps them understand Bill better, so they can teach and challenge him more effectively. If Bill doesn't go to church, this copy goes to a responsible church visitor in Bill's neighborhood, who invites Bill to continue learning about the Lord during the rest of the year. The third copy of the camper evaluation form is retained by the camp. If Bill goes to camp next year, it will help Bill's new counselor pick up where you left off. Be sure to write these summaries while the campers' accomplishments and decisions are still fresh in your mind.

Try to make your comments brief and positive. Frank may seem to have been incorrigible to you but next year he may be altogether different, or next year's counselor may be better able to reach him. Do not write statements on Frank's records that might prejudice another counselor, but write those helpful suggestions which you have found to work.

Planning ahead:

There may be inventories to take after the campers leave. And you may be responsible for that last cleanup and the closing of your cabin. Know what your responsibilities are in these areas.

You may be able to give helpful suggestions regarding next year's program, site, facilities, equipment, and scheduling.

Your director may ask you to evaluate your precamp training program, in order to improve it for next year. So think creatively during your weeks of counseling. Be as objective as you can in giving suggestions for improvement.

Follow-up:

After that last camper has waved good-bye, camp will be a mighty lonely place. But your job still is not through. There is follow-up.

Follow-up begins while camp is in session. It began by leading Joe into the Word of God after he made a decision for Christ. You started your follow-up work when you helped Jill study the Word of God for herself, or when you helped Jerry experience a meaningful quiet time with his Lord.

Maybe you started your campers in a Scripture memorization plan. Or perhaps you had them write letters to themselves about their decisions. (Don't be tempted to break the seals and read these, but be sure to mail them to your campers in the fall or just before Christmas.)

But now that they have gone, what can you do? Write! Things that may seem insignificant to you loom big to campers. So take time to write; show them you care. If you had so many campers that it is impossible to write them all, try a mimeographed letter. You can add a line at the bottom to personalize it for each camper.

Encourage Dave in his quiet time, in witnessing in school, and in taking part in the work of his church. Continue to show an interest in the problems of his home, in his school activities, and in his hobbies.

Girl campers enjoy a round-robin letter. You write to Jean; she adds a paragraph and sends it to Sue, who adds a paragraph and sends it to Mary, etc.

In your letter share personal blessings, but don't preach.

Recall times together. Campers enjoy getting a photo or two of camp.

You'd do well to remember your campers' birthdays. Alert counselors send cards on the anniversaries of their campers' second, or spiritual, birthdays as well.

You may be able to send or loan campers some good books. Send pertinent magazine articles and booklets. A subscription to a quiet-time guide or to a Christian magazine is well worthwhile, if you or the camp can afford it. You can also recommend good books, records, devotional helps, radio broadcasts, rallies, and special meetings.

Remember that you as a counselor are the key to effective follow-up. You already know Jack. You know his problems, his background, and you are aware of his needs. You may want to enroll him, or encourage him to enroll, in a Bible correspondence course.

If distance permits, plan a reunion of your cabin group during Thanksgiving weekend, the Christmas holidays, or spring vacation. This can be in a home if the group isn't too big, at a church, or better yet at the campsite itself if cold-weather facilities are available.

Campers appreciate phone calls, or even a visit if possible. Encourage your campers with suggestions on how to succeed in their Christian lives. Help them stand up for Christ in their everyday living.

If a camper lacks Christian contacts, refer him to a believer who lives near him, to someone who can take an interest in him.

A picture of the camp staff on a Christmas card, or a picture of camp in the snow, is another welcome follow-up.

You may get a letter from the camper you least expected would write. Some letters may show appreciation. Other campers may want to share problems with you and ask for advice. You can be their counselor long after camp.

Some may keep in touch for years. Be thankful to the Lord for entrusting you with the opportunity of touching young lives.

Counseling campers for Christ is a privilege—and a responsibility. Will you be a clear channel, allowing God to work through you, to accomplish His purposes in young lives? If you will, He will "by His mighty power at work within [you]... do far more than [you] would ever dare to ask or even dream of—infinitely beyond [your] highest prayers, desires, thoughts, or hopes" (Eph. 3:20, TLB).

Happy camping!

2
You —A Part of Camping History

People have always camped. It could be said that Adam and Eve had to do some survival camping when they were put out of the Garden of Eden. We read of Abraham's moving and pitching his tent (Gen. 13:4-8). Moses might be considered the director of a very large travel camp. Elijah did some survival camping by the Brook Cherith, and David camped out with his sheep.

Camping is also a part of our American heritage. The American Indians practiced many camping skills and were experts in hunting, fishing, and tracking. When the Pilgrims landed at Plymouth, Massachusetts in 1620, they recorded in their log that they "would go ashore and select a campsite." Settlers in the wilderness country depended on God and their camping skills to survive. Living intimately with the outdoors, they built their cabins, made their tools, cleared the ground, planted crops, and lived off the land. The Midwest and the West opened up due, in part, to outdoorsmen such as Daniel Boone, Kit Carson, Lewis and Clark, and the prairie pioneers.

Early farm life was rugged. Children living and working on farms were familiar with plants, animals, and the woods or wilderness. Social life centered around the family, neighbors, and the church.

The old-time camp meeting, a revival meeting held under a large canvas tent pitched on someone's farmland, was in many ways the forerunner of today's church camp. Families would come from miles around by horse and wagon or early model car to spend the day or days. The large meeting tent held wooden benches, and sawdust was spread on the ground. The day began early in the morning with prayers before breakfast, and meetings were held all morning, afternoon, and evening. Often, in the evening, a long evangelistic message was given, and "hitting the sawdust trail" was the term used when converts responded to the lengthy invitation.

By 1930, the trend was toward a more permanent campground and this gave rise to the Bible conference. Cabins and dorms were built. A permanent tabernacle, a dining hall, and kitchen were added. Recreational facilities, though frowned on at first, became a part of the permanent site. Canteens and bookstores carrying Christian literature became part of the Bible conference. Swimming pools were added to those conference grounds not on a lake.

The conference-camp format became one of meetings all morning, recreation in the afternoon, and an evangelistic service at night. Children's meetings followed the same pattern. A complex of facilities meant that entire families could camp at the same time in the same area with different programs for different age-groups. At some camps boys and girls were separated; other camps were coed. Despite early opposition, the Christian camp movement has flourished, and today is one of the fastest-growing segments of camping in America.

The First Camps

Secular camping dates its beginning from 1861 when Frederick William Gunn, the father of organized camping, founded the Gunnery School for Boys in Connecticut. At this school camp the boys marched, drilled, and slept out under the stars.

The first private camp was conducted in 1876 by Dr. Joseph Rothrock, a physician in Pennsylvania. He took frail boys into the outdoors and built them up physically. He had 20 campers his first year and operated camp from June through October.

The first church camp is credited to the Rev. George W. Hinkley of West Hartford, Connecticut. Mr. Hinkley camped with boys from his church in order to get to know them better in an informal setting. From this beginning in 1880, he later founded the Good Will Farm for Boys in Maine. He had services in the morning, sports in the afternoon, and talks or entertainment in the evening.

Camp Chocorua, the first private camp established to meet specific educational needs, was held in 1880 in New Hampshire. Dr. Ernest Balch took boys from well-to-do families to provide a worthwhile summer for them. Because Dr. Balch desired that his campers have a sense of responsibility and an appreciation for work, they worked in crews and did all the maintenance work of the camp. Recognition was given to outstanding campers, and all campers wore the camp uniform.

The first institutional camp was Camp Dudley, a YMCA camp founded in 1885 near Newburgh, New York. Though it was not named Camp Dudley until after the death of Sumner Dudley in 1897, it is the oldest organized camp still in existence.

Professor Arey of Rochester, New York established a camp for boys in 1892 which was later used as a girls' camp. In 1902, Camp Kehonka in New Hampshire became the first camp founded specifically for girls.

The Growth of Secular Camping

The camping movement has been said to have gone through several stages in its growth, though the stages are general with no clear dates for beginnings or endings.

Recreational Stage (about 1860-1920). Camps in this period provided healthy living in the open. Rugged outdoor life was thought to help campers grow physically. High morals and good character development were important. Usually camps were built around the founder and his personality. Well-known athletes, whose popularity was more important than their understanding of campers and camping, were brought to camp to attract campers.

Educational Stage (1920-1930). Progressive education began to affect the schools and this also had an effect on camps. There was an emphasis on the individual, and expressive activities such as music, art, drama, crafts, and creative writing were introduced into camp programs. Counselors now were given training and were chosen for their skills rather than their popularity in the sports arena.

Social Orientation Stage (beginning about 1930). Camp literature became available and camp personnel became more health- and safety-conscious during this period. Early morning dips and exercises before breakfast were not found to be beneficial to everyone. Small-group living and social adjustment were emphasized.

Democratic Stage (beginning about 1940). As our American democratic principles were being questioned and World War II was being waged, camps began to emphasize the democratic process. Campers became more involved in program planning, and camper councils supplied input for programs, discipline, and other phases of camp administration. Many camps were decentralized, which meant that programs were geared more to children's needs rather than forcing them into a regimented camp program.

Survival Camping (beginning in the 1960s). In a period of affluence there has come a return to the primitive, wilderness camping—canoe and backpacking trips, living a simple, uncomplicated life, and practicing the skills of our forefathers. (The need to preserve natural resources, to value wildlife, and to see the importance of each living thing in the ecological balance is something we've learned as a result.)

The Growth of Christian Camping

The early evangelical camps followed the Bible conference format with meetings every morning in a large tabernacle or meeting place, afternoons free for recreation, and a meeting every evening. Cabin devotions were held morning and evening in the large cabins or dormitories which housed the campers. The few, often untrained counselors sometimes worked on other camp jobs as well, but slept in the cabins with campers at night. Their main duties were to maintain order among the campers during the day and to see that they were in at night. Point systems and team competition helped promote participation in Bible reading and camp activities.

Evangelical camps have changed more slowly than secular camps and church camping tends to lag behind in its developmental stages. This is not necessarily bad. Perhaps we wait for new ideas to prove worthy, or search for a biblical principle for support. In any event, when it was recognized that the needs of individual campers were important, counselor training became a prerequisite. Instruction in the skills of camping—swimming, canoeing, riflery, campcraft, etc.—replaced a program of entertainment. Instead of having to participate in a highly competitive program, campers could choose many of their activities. Though much emphasis on sports remained, fine arts and crafts of all kinds became an important part of camp. Individual progress reports were kept; thus, campers competed against their own previous records.

Regular curriculum taught in small groups replaced the large all-camp Bible lectures, and periods of Bible study and campfires replaced the morning and evening meetings. More emphasis was placed on the cabin counselor and his personal contact with campers than on the platform ministry of the Bible teacher. The counselor who lived and played with the camper also taught the Bible study to his cabin group. His influence on the camper was considered to be more valuable than the big-name athlete. The evangelistic purpose switched from mass appeal to a personal approach.

Organizations Serving the Camping Movement

The American Camping Association (ACA) was founded in 1935 following the merger of several camping organizations.

Headquartered in Bradford Woods, Martinsville, Indiana, it has since grown to more than 2,400 member camps and an estimated 3.5 million employees, and publishes *Camping* magazine, a periodical which has done much to raise the standards and professional level of camping. The ACA certifies camps which meet its standards in administration, site, facilities, personnel, equipment, health, safety, transportation, and sanitation. It certifies camp directors and has developed leadership-training programs in camping skills. The organization also sponsors workshops and conventions, and lobbies for legislation affecting camping.

Christian Camping International, Wheaton, Illinois came into being in 1951 following the merger of five (three Eastern, one Midwestern, and one West Coast) camping associations. It publishes the *Journal of Christian Camping* and conducts regional as well as international workshops and biannual conventions. Its Foundations for Excellence, a certification program, outlines standards in the area of spiritual emphasis in addition to site, program, and personnel.

Trends in Camping Today

As you counsel this summer, you may become aware of some of the following trends taking place in your camp:

- Decentralization
- Younger campers going to camp (average age seems to be younger)
- Better qualified staff (you are one of them)
- Camping experiences for all age-groups
- Higher camping standards
- Indigenous activities
- More camping literature
- More democratic planning—more camper involvement in program; campers able to choose from many activities
- More interest in survival and stress camping
- More flexible programming—less structure, more leisurely pace
- More special interest camps—school, science, foreign language, music, sports, etc.
- More adequate sites
- More appreciation of nature and concern for ecology
- More emphasis on education in camp and less on recreation per se

More emphasis on outdoor skills
More personal counseling taking place
Less competitive programs
More use of year-round facilities
More balance in program (active-quiet, elementary-advanced) and more variety in program—backpacking, horseback trips, etc.
More concern for health and safety
More local, state, and federal participation in camp operation and legislation
More family camping with facilities for tents, trailers, or motor homes
More cooperative exchange of camping know-how among evangelicals
More special camping programs introduced such as Campers in Training, Leaders in Training, Counselor Aids, Teen Training Corps, Engineers, and Junior Counselors
More colleges extending credit to students involved in camp work
Colleges setting up laboratory camps for their Education and Christian Education majors
Camps contacting schools to enable them to offer college credit to their summer staffs

As you counsel this summer, see how many of these trends you can observe in your camp. Remember, you play an important part in the camping movement.

3
You and the Camp

Know the Philosophy of Your Camp

Don't let this term scare you. Philosophy, as discussed here, just means why your camp does what it does. It includes your camp leaders' beliefs, concepts, and attitudes. Your camp should have its philosophy written down. Be sure you understand it and can agree with it, for this will be a guide to your decision-making later on.

Is your camp a *conference* type of camp or a *counselor-centered* type of camp? Perhaps it is somewhere in between.

If your camp operates on a conference pattern, the whole camp may get together for several meetings in the morning and have the afternoon free for recreation. This may be followed by a service in the evening. Usually the whole camp does the same things at the same time.

The following chart shows a comparison between the two types of camp.

Centralized (conference type)	**Decentralized** (counselor-centered)
Bible taught by a platform speaker	Bible taught to cabin group by counselor
Conference type of program	Camp-oriented program
Structured program	More flexible and spontaneous program

Centralized	Decentralized
All-camp activities	Small-group activities
More spectator events	More camper participation
More emphasis on mass evangelism	More emphasis on personal evangelism
Program planned by administration	More cooperative and democratic planning by campers and staff
Fast tempo of camp	More leisurely pace
May be highly competitive	Camper competes against his own performance rather than against other campers
Usually more sports-oriented in free time	More emphasis on outdoor living and camping skills
May have autocratic leadership	More democratic leadership
Short camping periods—repeat same program	Can have longer camping periods —more variety in program offerings
Counselors have little training—mostly disciplinarians	Counselors better trained to counsel since program depends on them
Largely entertainment of campers	Seeks involvement of campers
Campers listen to speakers	Campers involved in direct Bible study

If your campers have some choices of activities but still follow a fixed schedule, you probably have a semidecentralized camp. Because different activities are going on at the same time, a semidecentralized camp lies somewhere in between the two extremes. Though there may be some preplanned large-group activities, many activities are conducted in small groups, with more flexibility of schedule and more emphasis on campers' needs.

Many Christian camps today have moved away from the strongly *centralized* type of camping. This doesn't suggest that one type is right and the other is wrong; they are just different philosophies of camping.

Knowing your own camp's philosophy will help you understand the *why* of your camp program, for it is an outgrowth of your camp leaders' philosophy. It makes a difference whether or not the whole camp goes on a hike every Thursday, or whether you can take your own cabin group out to explore a stream, though it isn't on the schedule. It makes a difference as to whether camp activities such as swimming, horseback riding, and archery are viewed as bait to recruit campers or whether they are looked on as opportunities for campers to learn and practice Christian principles.

Biblical principles affect a Christian camp's philosophy, which, in turn, affects its program. Here are examples of how this works in some camps:

Biblical Principle	Camp Philosophy	Implication for Program
"Do not merely listen to the word. . . . Do what it says" (James 1:22).	Camp is a laboratory where Christian living is tested.	Campers are given opportunities through cabin activities to practice truths learned.
Christ deals with individual needs (John 3—4).	A counselor's personal contact with each camper is important.	There is provision for small-group activities, and personal counseling. There's a low camper-counselor ratio.
Jesus demonstrated an integrated personality. He grew in wisdom, stature, and favor with God and man (Luke 2:52).	A Christian should not consider some of his activities spiritual, others secular.	The spiritual emphasis is felt throughout the day, not only during Bible studies and other meetings.
Jesus worked with all His disciples. He did not designate one as greatest in His kingdom.	Personal growth of every camper is important, not recognition of one or two outstanding campers.	Achievement recognition is given to each camper rather than to the "best" camper or "best" athlete.
"Do your best to present yourself to God as one approved, a workman . . . who correctly handles the word of truth" (2 Tim. 2:15).	Instead of giving pat answers, counselors guide campers into finding answers to their problems in God's Word.	During quiet times and cabin devotional times counselors help campers discover God's truths for themselves.

Know the Objectives of Your Camp

Your camp director will probably send you materials to read before you go to camp. You may have lessons to complete and books to study. Sometime after you have been accepted on the staff and before camp opens, you should become familiar with your camp's aims. Your camp's goals may be similar to these:

Physical Objectives

To provide for healthy physical growth
To help campers develop good health habits (cleanliness, proper rest, balanced diet, exercise, and proper care of their bodies as God's temples)
To provide a program graded to campers' abilities and interests
To provide an atmosphere conducive to good mental health and free from tension

Social Objectives

To provide profitable experience in Christian community living (unselfishly getting along with others)
To provide an opportunity for each camper to make a contribution to the group
To help campers make profitable use of leisure time
To develop a spirit of comradeship
To accept other campers from different backgrounds and of different races
To learn to be cooperative and to respect others' property
To develop a sense of social responsibility
To develop the ability to function in a democratic society
To provide Christian fellowship and friendships
To gain an appreciation of the contribution of others
To learn how to get along with people of different temperaments
To help campers learn leadership skills
To help campers feel at home in the outdoors

Personal Development Objectives

To help campers make right decisions and to accept the consequences of wrong decisions
To stimulate creativity and independence
To increase understanding and appreciation of God's creation
To learn basic camping skills
To develop a sense of self-worth

To develop a variety of skills which may be useful in adult life
To help campers develop inner controls along with freedom from parental controls
To help campers to think, analyze, judge, and make wise choices
To develop a keener sense of beauty
To learn to be good stewards of God's creation (conserve the natural resources)
To help campers develop leadership skills
To provide time for campers to be alone and evaluate their own goals and achievements

Spiritual Objectives

To lead each camper who does not know Christ to receive Him as his or her personal Saviour
To help each camper grow in the Lord during camp through increased knowledge of God's Word, through developing good habits of Christian living, including a devotional time in the Word and prayer each day
To help campers develop Christ-centered personalities
To give vocational guidance by making campers aware of the need for Christians in all occupations, especially in the fields of foreign and domestic Christian education
To guide campers toward maturity in Christ
To encourage spiritual decisions at each camper's level of readiness
To counsel campers as individuals in the areas of their spiritual needs
To develop Christian leadership skills that can be used in their local churches when they return from camp

Remember that your campers will have their own reasons for coming to camp. Jim may tell you that he came to camp to learn to swim. Mary came to be with her friends; Judy came to make new friends. Bob came to go on a canoe trip and get away from the city. All of your campers came to have *fun*! Try to see that each of your campers has his objectives fulfilled at camp.

Parents also have objectives. If you talk with Mrs. Smith she may tell you that she wants Patty to learn to make her bed and pick up her things. Or Rick's dad wants him to learn respect for the rights of others. Other parents may tell you:

I want him to come home healthier and stronger.
I want him to gain (or lose) weight.
I want him to learn to behave.

I want him to learn some skill—to ride a horse, shoot, be at home in the outdoors.
I want him to learn to share.
I want him to grow in the Lord.

All parents are trusting you with the health and safety of their offspring. They want to be sure that you will take a personal interest in their sons and daughters, that you will care for their needs—and that you will be an example worthy of following.

Is this a big order? Do you feel inadequate? You are—in yourself. But if you trust and obey God, He will "supply all that you need from His glorious resources in Christ Jesus" (Phil. 4:19, PH). Near the end of camp your director will give you a camper evaluation form (see p. 205) to enable you to evaluate camp in terms of how well these aims and objectives were met.

Know the Organizational Structure of Your Camp

Where do you fit into the structure of the whole camp? What is the chain of command? To whom do you go with a problem? To whom are you directly responsible? Each camp has its own organizational setup to meet its own needs. Perhaps the individuals who report to your director are those in charge of program, food, maintenance, finances, and health. Here's a typical organizational chart:

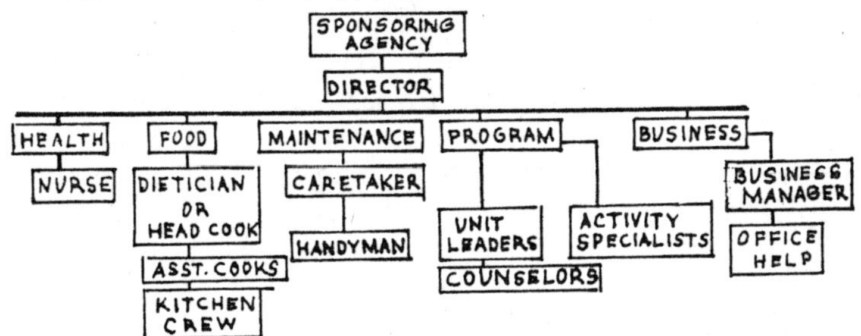

The size of your camp, the ages of the campers, the program offered, and the type of camp will affect your chart's structure.

Did you receive a job analysis (or job description) in the mail? (There is a sample job analysis on p. 202.) A job analysis tells you who your boss is and what your general and specific duties are. Add this form to your counselor manual, if you have one, or tuck it in the folder of things you will be taking to camp. Read it over carefully. If you have any questions, write or phone your director *before* camp begins.

Your counselor job analysis or counselor agreement will spell out your responsibilities and the camp's responsibilities, respectively. If there is any remuneration, this is stated in the agreement. Your insurance coverage, paid by your camp (such as health and accident or workman's compensation) is also included. Any compensation to you for traveling or laundry expenses is mentioned. The date you are expected at camp and the date when you will leave are included. Assignments or preparation for teaching may be included as part of your responsibility. Attendance at counselor-training sessions may also be written into your contract. (For a sample agreement, see p. 203.)

Remember, a signed contract is your word of honor that you will fulfill all your obligations.

Know the History of Your Camp

Your director or camp owner will be glad to tell you how your camp was started. He may tell you about it during your first day on the campsite or perhaps during a winter precamp training session. Many camp directors or owners have a thrilling story to tell of how the Lord provided the property or how He indicated that this was His work. Try to catch your camp founder's vision. Ralph Waldo Emerson once said that an organization is but the lengthened shadow of a man. What man, what circumstances, what needs, what unusual events helped bring your camp into existence? This summer you will be a special part of this work!

Know the Traditions of Your Camp

Over the years every camp develops some traditions that are uniquely its own. An important sense of belonging can be created as veteran campers pass your camp's traditions on to new campers. Returning campers look forward to certain informal ceremonies and traditions, which give them a sense of security and self-identification. Such customs should be meaningful and help further your camp's aims.

The traditions of your camp may include a special campfire, initiation ceremonies, a unique birthday celebration, a midnight hike, or going to Sunday School at a nearby country church. Special days may become traditional—Circus Day, Christmas (with caroling after taps), Olympic Day, or a Counselor-Camper Day (when campers and counselors trade places).

The special use of a certain location in camp can lead to traditions, such as a Story Tree where, during free hours, a counselor spins yarns. Sunrise Hill may be a place set aside for an Easter sunrise service once during camp. You may have a Pit of Oblivion where old jokes or inappropriate songs are buried with ceremony by the whole camp.

Special names for cabins, washhouses, and chores may become traditional. A particular handshake, a special knock on the cabin door, or a farewell arch made with flags for campers leaving camp may have special significance. A special good-night song, a cabin song, or a camp song may bring back happy memories for your campers long after camp is over. Become acquainted with these traditions before camp and you will add to that intangible something called esprit de corps.

Know the Policies of Your Camp

Policies for camp counselors constitute regulations within which they have safety and freedom. Your leaders have previously thought through and anticipated areas needing clarification. These policies may concern proper attire (you'll want to know this before you pack for camp), use of the telephone, mail procedures, time off, mealtime procedures, Sunday dress, cleanup routines, and dating regulations among staff members. Some camps limit the traveling distance on your day off (if you drive hundreds of miles you probably won't come back refreshed for another week of responsibility).

What transportation is available for days off? What about the use of camp cars? Is there a charge? There is sometimes a policy concerning the borrowing of other staff members' cars, to protect a car owner from feeling obligated to loan his car. Is there a counselor curfew? Is it the same every night of the week? What about personal money? Is there a safe for valuables? Is there a counselor's kitchen? If so, what hours is it open? Is there any regulation regarding staff members latching onto pies or cakes left over from supper? Are laundry facilities available?

What are dishwashing procedures? Do campers wash or dry dishes or have any kitchen responsibilities? If so, what is the counselor's job at this time?

How and where do you get supplies? What are the proper procedures for ordering materials? Through what channels do you go to get food for a cookout?

What are the emergency procedures in case of fire, flood, tornado, or evacuation of camp?

What are your responsibilities during rest hour? Are you to be in your cabin with your campers? What should happen at this time?

Rules have reasons behind them. Find out what these are and talk over with your director any questions you may have. Remember that as a staff member you have an obligation to keep these policies, even when you think of some good reasons for not doing so.

Know Your Campsite

Look over that sketchy map which was sent to you. Locate the dining hall, the health center, your cabin, the washhouse, and the nature nook.

Become familiar with the general layout of the camp so you

can quickly locate fire equipment, first-aid equipment, water fountains, and overnight spots. Try to visit the campsite before camp, if pre-in-camp training is not held. A map of the surrounding area, on which any state parks and places of scenic or historic interest are marked, will help you in planning out-of-camp trips.

The U.S. Geological Survey, Washington, D.C. can supply you with topographical maps of most areas in the United States. These helpful maps pinpoint locations of buildings, lakes, streams, trails, wooded areas, marshes, rapids, falls, elevations, and contours. A study of one of these maps may challenge your campers to a cross-country hike, an exploration, or an orienteering trip with map and compass. A nearby trout stream, a clay bank, or a waterfall also provide opportunities for creative cabin activities. Perhaps you can visit and check out some of these places before your campers arrive.

Know the Opening-day Procedures of Your Camp

Be familiar with the opening-day program. A camper's first impression of camp is important. Be available to meet him—and his parents, if they come. A talk with Woody's parents often gives you insight into his behavior. Help Woody get unpacked; show him where to keep his things; how to make his bed properly with hospital corners. Introduce him to other campers. By the first meal try to know all of your campers in your cabin by their real names or by the nicknames they prefer. (Be wary of using nicknames such as Tubby, Fatso, Boneyard, or Crisco Kid. Your campers may be used to them, but deep inside they'd rather not be known for their appearance.) Every camper should have the security of his counselor knowing him by name the first day of camp.

On opening day some staff members may be assigned to meet incoming cars; others will take new campers to their cabins. Sometimes cookies and punch are provided for parents and tours of the campsite are led by older, returning campers. The whole staff should be on hand, neatly groomed, ready to help where needed.

Most camps have a well-planned procedure for new campers. From the parking area or from the bus, they are directed to the camp office where spending money is deposited and camp fees are paid (if they weren't collected before camp).

From here they may be directed to the health center, where the nurse collects each camper's medical examination form (if this has not been received previously). A short checkup is given by the nurse, and all medications are left with her. The excitement of coming to camp may cause a camper to run a slight temperature. A double check by the nurse can sometimes prevent the spread of colds or some childhood disease.

From here campers go to their cabins and change into camp clothing. Perhaps you can take your campers on a tour of the site, so they will know where to find the washhouse, the craft shop, the ball field, and the dining hall.

Let them know some of the exciting things in store for them during the week. Let them feel that theirs is the best cabin in camp. Challenge your charges to make it the cleanest cabin all week! Build respect and loyalty in your group. Go over with them the daily schedule, special events, and mealtime proce-

CAPER DUTY CHART

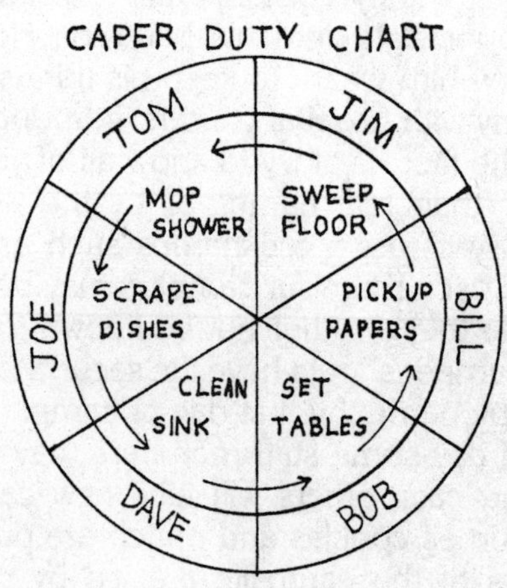

dures, but don't try to cover too much at one time. Allow time for them to talk and to share too.

Of course, you will have the cabin clean and inviting before your campers arrive. Decorating it with pine sprays and cones, or just a welcome sign on the bulletin board, adds a friendly touch. A schedule of coming events may be posted, along with procedures for fire drills, mail delivery, camp capers, and mealtimes. You will probably need to teach some campers good housekeeping. Right after breakfast is a good time for campers to straighten out their belongings, their cabins, and the grounds.

In some camps, campers help with various camp chores. Working together should help teach the appreciation and dignity of work and should be an enjoyable time of joking and singing, as all contribute as a group to camp living. Work should never be doled out as punishment (nor should Scripture memorization ever be given as punishment). Your own attitude toward work is important, for if you make a game of it, the campers will learn to enjoy it. Though your supervision may not be needed on chores, this should be a time of enjoying each other's company. It should not be "I'm here to see that you do the job right," but "Let's do this job quickly together."

Without words, you can teach that it is important to throw papers in the trash can. Dropping them on the ground only means picking them up later. You may want to make a rotating chart of camper duties for your cabin group (see chart on p. 40).

Work can be a fulfillment of a camper's needs. Even grubby, menial tasks can help build one's self-esteem and boost his security. Work can be made joyous and creative.

Know the Closing-day Procedures of Your Camp

Are you responsible for inventories? For cleaning up part of the camp? For lost and found? You may be asked to help take an inventory of sports equipment, craft and nature supplies, library books, tripping equipment, and canned food.

Of course you will leave your cabin clean, trash cans emptied, and flaps or windows closed. You may be asked to help strike and clean the tents, or store the canoes and bring in the dock.

Articles left behind are a bugaboo for any camp. Some camps mail back to a camper any marked clothing. Others keep lost-and-found articles for several weeks and then give them to a city mission or some other worthy cause. You may be asked to list these articles for the person who will be receiving letters after camp requesting Barry's Bible, Susan's sweater (size 10), and Jim's jacket.

4
Those Campers

The best way to get to know your campers is to be with them—no programming takes the place of personal contact. This was the Lord's method, for "He appointed twelve . . . that they might be with Him" (Mark 3:14). As you try to follow Christ's example, look for opportunities to walk to the beach with Dan, or to catch up with Tim on the way to the dining hall. Listen to your campers; observe their actions and reactions.

No two campers are exactly alike, nor will any list of characteristics fit them all. But it is good to know the general characteristics of a 12-year-old boy, and to know what to expect in general from a 15-year-old girl, even though two 15-year-olds will not be at the same point of development. Your camper may be a 14-year-old physically, a 16-year-old mentally, a 12-year-old emotionally, and a mere babe spiritually. There may not be one camper in your cabin who is "average." You must get to know your campers and that means spending time with them. See them as individuals. Accept them as they are, not as you wish they were. You will wish sometimes that you could see inside to know what makes them tick. You can't, but the Holy Spirit knows and understands them, and He can give you insights beyond your natural ability as you seek His guidance.

Basic Needs of Campers

A camper needs to feel *secure* and *wanted.* He must have a sense of belonging in your cabin group; he needs to be needed. Start by helping him make his bed, unpack, and put his things away. Then get him into an activity. This sense of belonging and involvement also goes a long way in avoiding the problem of camper homesickness.

A camper needs *recognition.* He wants to be recognized as an individual, not as one camper in 453. Know him by name by the first mealtime. Find something he can do well and praise him for it. Praise will go much further in getting your cabin cleaned than will scolding. The camper who is all thumbs in the craft shop may be able to win the 100-yard dash. The nonathlete may write a song about your cabin. Each needs recognition in some area and it is up to you to discover his proficiency.

A third need is for *new experiences.* Campers want to do in camp what they cannot do at home. Provide the distinctive camp activity and leave to the home, school, or church the things that can be done just as well in that environment. Campers love excitement. Primaries love surprises. Juniors like to be challenged with the difficult. Junior highs want a change from the common place, and senior highs thrive on excitement and daring. Camp ought to provide these experiences within the Christian framework and within the bounds of safety.

The fourth basic need is *involvement*—an opportunity for a camper to give himself to something big. Camp can provide a physically, mentally, and spiritually stretching experience. Campers can contribute something to your camp that others will enjoy. Stress programs will challenge a teen to do what he thought was impossible; but with the Lord's help, he is able to scale that wall or climb that mountain.

Age Characteristics

Here is a list of general characteristics. (For more details see the books listed in the Bibliography, pp. 207-213.)

Primary Campers (ages 6-8)

Physically
Growth relatively slow but steady
Big muscles developing
Fatigues easily
Needs about 11 hours sleep
Often restless

Mentally
Thinks in terms of the present
Has a good imagination
Is literal-minded
Has great curiosity
Is beginning to read, print, and write

Socially
Talkative
Enjoys playing with his friends
Plays low-organization games
Likes to be with adults and may copy them

Emotionally
May be impatient
Emotions easily stirred
May daydream and procrastinate
Still dependent on adults
May be bossy

Spiritually
Can pray and expect God to answer
May be ready to accept Jesus Christ
Wants to be good and please God
May be curious about heaven or death
Is learning obedience to God and his parents
Can read his Bible and begin to have his own quiet time

Junior Camper (ages 9-11)

Physically
Strong, healthy, active
Likes the out-of-doors
Needs 10-10½ hours of sleep
Slow growth
A few girls reach puberty

Mentally
Reads well
Memorizes easily
Collects things and facts
Acquires more information than he understands
Great curiosity
Has reasoning ability
Often talkative

Socially
Healthy respect for authority
Hero-worshiper
Demands justice and fairness
Likes a gang or club
May be indifferent or antagonistic to opposite sex
Competitive spirit
Enjoys teamwork

Emotionally
Dislikes outward display of affection
Enjoys slapstick humor
Is developing a value system
Little control of emotions, but

controls are developing

Spiritually

Capable of making decision for Christ
Does not want to show emotion
Has questions—accepts adult answers
Ideals are being formed
Concerned for the lost
Can have quiet time

A junior camper is a doer. He is always running, jumping, sliding, wrestling, or fighting. He likes the rough and tumble for the sheer pleasure of activity. He loves camp and all of its activities except showers, rest hour, and going to bed. He can take care of his clothes, but he usually doesn't. You may have to make sure that he changes his underwear and puts on a clean T-shirt, or he may go home with a suitcase full of clean clothes, having worn the same ones all week. Girls may not have the same problem, but they leave camp without Bibles, sweaters, and jackets and you may be sending things to Jeannie or Pam all summer.

Camp was made for the junior, it seems. He loves the hikes, nature study (you may find his collection of "critters" between your sheets some night!), outdoor cooking, explorations, campfires, fishing, swimming, and other sports.

He is usually ready to receive Christ at junior age if he hasn't already done so. He knows what sin is, and readily acknowledges that he is a sinner. He can understand that Christ took his punishment in his place.

Junior High Campers (ages 12-14)

Physically

Rapid, uneven growth
Low endurance
Puberty—girls develop sooner than boys
May appear awkward; voice changes

Mentally

Ability to memorize increases (memorization should be meaningful)
Likes adventure and discovery
Imagines himself a hero—daydreams
Thinks he knows everything
Makes snap judgments

Needs 9½-10 hours of sleep

Socially

Attracted to the opposite sex
Belongs to a gang
Wants to be grown-up
Has "crushes" on favorite adults
Wants to be independent of adults
Desires approval of the group
Hero-worshiper
Desires both solitude and society
Needs recognition, love, patience
Needs the security of authority

Strong sense of humor, often uncontrolled

Emotionally

Emotions fluctuate—hard to control
Feels misunderstood
Self-conscious
Wants to be treated as an adult

Spiritually

May doubt miracles, but hopes for the miraculous
Basic beliefs of childhood may break down
May doubt God's love for him
Periods of readiness to accept Christ
Wants to do something for the Lord
Can begin habits of Bible study and quiet time

This age has been called the stress period of life. Junior highs are neither children nor adults. Due to their rapid growth, they often suffer fatigue after periods of extreme energy. Both guys and girls at this age often appear awkward and unpoised, and they need to understand themselves. Their appetites are large at a time when he may be fighting acne and she may be trying to lose weight. Their attitudes change frequently. The eager-beaver camper of last year may appear to be nonchalant and indifferent to everything this year. He is extremely peer conscious and his gang influences his dress, attitudes, language, habits, and viewpoints. He appears to know everything and is afraid to let you know there is anything he doesn't know.

He may doubt God's love for him. He may ask, "If God loves me, why did He let my mother die?" or "Why doesn't God stop war?" He begins to reevaluate his childhood concepts, and he may start to question Scripture. "Why don't we see miracles like this today?" He is internalizing and personalizing his beliefs, and this is good. Guide him in thinking through his doubts. A junior high camper may not know the Lord's will for his life. Encourage him to want God's will for his life, whatever that may be.

Questions about dating, drugs, drinking, and sex will come up in your cabin times. Be prepared to direct your campers to biblical principles; pat answers won't do. There are few absolutes in today's cultural or social moral standards, and the temptations confronting a teenager are frightening. He needs the indwelling power of the Holy Spirit, given at salvation, to live up to God's standards. The assurance that God wants to guide him daily can be an exciting and challenging discovery.

High School Camper

Physically

Looks mature
Keen senses—touch, smell
Time of experimentation (may try drugs, drinking)
Physical habits forming
Needs 8½-9 hours of sleep
Boys' metabolism rate exceeds that of girls; physical activity reduced for girls

Socially

Wants to be with the opposite sex
Cares about appearance
Conforms to group
Wants social approval
Rebels against authority
Interested in fads
Likes a crowd
Copies what he thinks is grown-up

Spiritually

May be indifferent to spiritual things
His beliefs are personal
May have many doubts

Mentally

Can see relationships
Remembers ideas better than words
Idealistic
Interested in the process of success
Can form opinions based on reasoning
Has a long memory span
Can see another's point of view

Emotionally

Wants a thrill
Emotions intense and fluctuating
Peer group sets emotional pattern
May keep feelings to himself
Influenced by successful professional people
Starts to develop a philosophy of life

His doubts may arise because he has not had his questions answered satisfactorily, or because he has seen inconsistencies in the lives of Christian adults. Because Christianity has not been related to his life-situations, he may wonder if it really works. He may doubt God's love because of ill health, or question why God permitted the death of a brother, sister, or parent. He may have been led to believe that once he received Christ as his Saviour, all his problems would be solved, and he hasn't found this to be true. He may have gone forward as a child in a meeting, or even joined a church, without meeting Christ. He may have been led into a false security that he was saved because he raised his hand during an invitation. Learn the reason for a camper's doubt and deal with it prayerfully.

Remember, each of your campers, regardless of age, will have these basic needs:

To love and be loved
To be recognized as a person
To make a contribution of his own—to be needed
To be free to inquire and know
To belong
To be free from guilt

Preventing Problems

The old proverb, "An ounce of prevention is worth a pound of cure" certainly applies to camp. When a camper is a "problem" it is usually because he has not had his needs fulfilled in a satisfactory way. When a problem arises with Danny, try to discover the cause, the "why" behind his actions, rather than merely dealing with the behavior which may be only the effect. If the camp program is not meeting your campers' needs, they may devise socially unacceptable ways to meet them.

Be positive in making suggestions to campers. Rather than *telling* them to clean the cabin, make a game of doing the job with them. Give praise and encouragement.

Instead of listing the camp rules, call them "Suggestions for Campers" and give them the reasons for such regulations. A notice posted in the cabin might look like this:

To the Campers in Lone Pine Cabin

For our safety, we don't leave the campgrounds without a counselor. Because we need rest and sleep for the busy day ahead, we are quiet and in bed by 10:00 PM.

Make suggestions positively, conveying the idea, "This is what we do here," rather than "These are camp rules one, two, three—and any offenders will be sent home." To a belligerent camper, this is almost a challenge.

A camper may misbehave because he resents inconsistent discipline, or because he feels forced to conform against his will. Unacceptable behavior may also be compensation for feelings of inferiority or lack of recognition.

If the program is too tightly scheduled and overdemanding, discipline problems may result. On the other hand, if the program does not make enough demands on your campers' energies, you will find them planning escapades after taps, or seeking other outlets for their pent-up vitality.

You may feel like "telling off" the loud braggart in your cabin, but he may be unconsciously trying to hide his sense of insecurity and inadequacy. Try to understand the "why" behind his actions. Even though you'd like to cut him down to size, this might be the wrong thing to do and only increase his compulsion to brag.

Unmet needs may be the cause of behavior such as: poor eating, thumb-sucking, bed-wetting, masturbation, nail-biting, restless sleeping, speech problems, crying, poor concentration, nervousness, fear, daydreaming, stubbornness, lethargy, teasing, fighting, bullying, lying, stealing, temper tantrums, and destructiveness.

"Problem campers" are often the products of problem homes. An overindulgent or overprotective parent may have given a camper so much attention that he is bothered because he is not the center of attention at camp. On the other hand, a camper who has been neglected may believe that he has been sent to camp so his parents could vacation by themselves. Both of these campers may demonstrate problem behavior.

Habits of a lifetime do not change overnight. Growth is usually a gradual process. But this does not excuse you from responsibility to your camper with a problem. Even in a week's time you can see changes in attitude and behavior, if a camper lets God work in his life. Commit each camper to the Lord. Be sure you are a clear channel through which God has the freedom to work.

Special Camper Problems

Timid Timothy:

The timid, shy camper in your cabin needs to be drawn into the group. His behavior may result from a combination of several causes. Is he afraid others will laugh at his suggestions? Is he insecure? Tim may be an unhappy camper who wants desperately to belong. Discover his interests or talents and use them for the good of the group. Do things with him. Help him achieve in the eyes of his tentmates.

Alibi Albert:

He is your camper who always finds someone or something on which to blame his failures. (Most of us are guilty of this at times.) He lost the checker game because his opponent cheated. He failed his swim test because the water was too cold. His team lost in baseball because the umpire was blind. Help Albert see himself objectively and help him take responsibility for his mistakes. Let him know that you care about him, win or lose.

Bill Bully:

You are likely to have him in your cabin too. Why does he act this way? What does he really need? Your first impulse is to take him down a peg. But wait a minute. Maybe it is his insecurity that makes him pick on little Ken or brag about his brother's cabin cruiser. Give him the recognition he needs when he works cooperatively with the group. Ignore his bids for attention before others. Establish rapport and be patient with him. Remember how patient the Lord has been with you.

Susie Show-off:
Like Bill Bully, she may be hiding a sensitive, lonely heart under that noisy outside. She may be finding security for herself in minimizing the accomplishments of others. Be understanding. Encourage trust. Give credit for a behind-the-scenes job that is well done. Give recognition whenever she does the right thing, so she won't need to try so hard to be noticed.

Temper-tantrum Tommy:
Temper tantrums, stubbornness, and rebellion may be habits of behavior which have brought about desired results at home or at school. Tommy is using a method which has worked before to secure a desired goal. Ignore his displays of temper. Remove him from his audience and leave him alone when he throws a tantrum. Give recognition for helpful, unselfish behavior.

Homesick Harry:
A camper who has never been away from home before or who has been overly dependent on a parent may face many fears in new surroundings. He may have received no letters from home, or (worse yet) letters that tell how much he is missed and all the things he is missing by being at camp. If Harry feels that his being sent to camp is a rejection by his parents, this may lead to homesickness. Home conditions, illness at home, uncertainties, or family problems will influence a camper's adjustment to camp.

Watch for signs of homesickness. The camper who stays by himself, does not participate in camp activities, cries easily, shows a lack of interest and enthusiasm in camp, and spends much time writing letters is probably homesick. Homesickness is most evident during the quieter times in the camp schedule—meals, rest hour, bedtime, or on a Sunday (especially if this is your first day of camp). Harry is less likely to be homesick if he is kept busy in activities, has responsibility, and is accepted and feels needed by his cabinmates. Never make fun of a homesick camper. Let him know that many people have felt as he does. Let him talk it over. Try to find the reason for his feelings. Does he like his cabin, his counselor, his cabinmates? Is there some physical problem that could be helped by the camp nurse? Has he heard from home? Is he worried about something? Sometimes finding an adult as a parent-substitute will help. Perhaps he can be put with a counselor whom he likes and can help that counselor all morning. Encourage him to accept separation from home as a part of growing up.

Encourage him to try camp for at least a few days. If he goes home right away, he will not be giving camping a fair trial. If he is a Christian, you may challenge him to not miss the Lord's purposes for bringing him to camp.

To stay and overcome homesickness may become a real spiritual victory. On the other hand, it may be better to let a camper leave than to infect other campers with the germ of homesickness. Perhaps your director will give him permission to call home or go home after he has given camp a few days' trial. If you do promise this, be sure to keep your word.

Every camper needs love, acceptance, and security. An unloved camper can better comprehend God's love if he sees that love demonstrated in your life. As Jim Vaus says, "When love is felt, the message is heard."

Will you present Jesus Christ in this way?

Setting Goals

On the first or second day of camp set specific, realistic goals which you want to see accomplished in the life of each of your campers during his stay with you. Write them down.

Your goals may read something like these:

Tim and George—salvation
Wayne—victory over his temper

Hank—overcome self-centeredness
Steve—break up relationship with unsaved girl friend
Jim—recognize the claims of Christ in every area of life

Plan your cabin activities with these goals in mind. If you are leading the Bible study with your campers, your written goals will guide you as you prepare. Plan to spend some time alone with each camper each week. If this is casual, all the better. Talk with him about his interests, his purposes in life (if he is an older camper), and his relationship to the Lord. Take advantage of unscheduled contacts—along the trail to Lookout Point, on the way to the beach. There will be opportunities if you look for them and there will be the whole world of nature at your doorstep for illustrations.

Commit each camper to the Lord. Remember, God is far more interested in your Sam and Bill than you could ever be. Trust Him to work in each life this camp period—and watch the results.

Last year's camp evaluation form (see p. 205) may provide you with helpful information. A permanent record card on each camper, if kept from year to year, is a useful tool when a returning camper is new to you.

Negative information may prejudice you against a camper before he arrives. Remember that a camper can change during the year. Accept him for what he is this year. Keep this in mind when you record a camper's progress at the end of camp.

Your campers should not have to face the stigma of this summer's misdemeanors next summer. Record what will be helpful and give insight to another counselor next year, but not minor behavior deviations which may have bothered you.

Campers Are Always Learning

Campers learn camping skills such as swimming, canoeing, sailing, tripping, cooking out, and woodsmanship by doing them, but all of their learning does not take place in scheduled class periods. For example, they learn to get along together, and to take responsibility in the cabin by living together. They learn socially acceptable behavior as they work together on projects. They learn leadership skills as they serve on committees and play on teams.

Truth learned must be put into practice or it isn't really learned. Camp is a proving ground where spiritual truths are tested and practiced during camp's many activities. It provides campers with opportunities to relate Christian principles to behavior on the ball field, the tennis court, the waterfront, and in the craft shop. What are they learning in your cabin?

Campers want to repeat satisfying experiences. If they have had a good overnight, they will want to go again. But if Johnny's sleeping bag got soaking wet in the rain, and supper was burned, and the canoe upset, it may be difficult to arouse interest in another overnight. So plan carefully and try to make your campers' experiences worthwhile and enjoyable.

Campers learn by example. "The only letter I need is you yourselves!" (2 Cor. 3:2, TLB) You are teaching by example all day long. Campers watch you like hawks. An unkind word or an off-color jest will not be missed by their ears. A word of griping or a critical remark will be overheard by some camper. They may mimic your gestures; they may copy your talk; they may even try to dress as you do. If you wear your sweat shirt inside out with sleeves torn off, watch how many campers will follow suit. If you go barefoot like Robinson Crusoe, watch how many stubbed toes and cut feet start coming to the nurse. Campers pick up your attitudes, your likes and dislikes. They are learning continually.

What are they learning from watching you? What are you really teaching them during cleanup time? Have they caught your attitude of "A half-done job is good enough," or have they learned the feeling of self-respect and pride that comes with a job well done? Even washing dirty dishes can be done well to please the Lord!

As you teach the Word of God, do you convey an attitude of "Let's get this over in a hurry so we can get out and have fun"? Or do you approach Bible study with expectancy—"What will

God say to us today through His Word?"

Be sure that your reflection of Jesus Christ before your campers is sharp and clear, not blurred by selfish interests or wrong motives. Campers will follow your example. Is it worth copying?

5
You and the Counseling Process

How Jesus Counseled

"These will be His royal titles: 'Wonderful,' 'Counselor,' 'the Mighty God' " (Isa. 9:6, TLB).

God's Son, Jesus Christ is the master Counselor. Learn His methods. Rely on the Holy Spirit to guide you. When you are sensitive to His leading, He will give you insights far deeper than your own.

Look at the Lord's dealings with the woman at the well (John 4). He opened the conversation. He made the approach. He began talking about something familiar to her—water. He identified with her. He involved her in conversation. He did not begin by condemning her, even though He knew all about her. Instead, He led her from well water to spiritual water. He related to her background.

When she talked of the hostility between the Jews and Samaritans, He waited until this emotional roadblock was gone. He brought her step-by-step to the point where she asked for His kind of water (4:15). Then He moved into the area of her sin without rejecting her. He clearly disagreed with what she had done, but took time in the heat of the day and from His busy schedule to deal with her problem. When she changed the subject, He led her in progressive steps to the point of insight. When she was ready, He revealed who He was.

Compare this chapter with John 3. Jesus dealt here with Nicodemus, a leader, a religious gentleman of good reputation. Nicodemus opened the conversation, and the Lord began on the level of Nicodemus' understanding. This man had a background far different from the woman of chapter 4. Jesus dealt with each person as an individual and moved at the counselee's pace. With Nicodemus, He began by talking of the new birth, not water. His words recorded in John 3:16-18 were not addressed to a large crowd, but to one man.

What do these two incidents teach you about how Christ values an individual?

How I May Counsel

Help each camper face himself squarely in the light of the Word of God. Help him assume responsibility for his problem and for making the right decisions. Be careful not to try to solve your camper's problems for him, but guide him into the Word of God where the Holy Spirit can speak to him and where he can find principles for making the right choices. Your campers cannot take you home with them after camp, to solve their problems all through the year. But they can take along Christ, who has promised never to leave or forsake His own (Heb. 13:5).

All problems do not have spiritual origins. A camper is a complex individual whose physical, emotional, mental, and social needs must be met, as well as his spiritual needs. But even though a camper's problem may not be basically spiritual, he will probably not find a permanent solution until he is in a proper relationship to Jesus Christ. Outside pressures may bring outer conformity, but there must be an inner response to bring about a genuine change. This inner changing is the work of the Holy Spirit in a life.

Some behavior problems are of a spiritual origin. Spiritual maladies may be the cause of homesickness, apparent disinterest in what's going on, aggressiveness, or running away from camp. As a wise counselor, you will try to find out why your camper is acting as he is. Rather than disciplining or treating a manifestation of behavior, seek its cause.

Perhaps you are saying, "But I won't be counseling any problem campers." By living with campers, by being with them through the day, you will be counseling. And everybody has some problems. It is not a question of whether or not you will counsel, but what kind of counseling you will be doing.

Helpful Steps in Counseling

Contact. Be sensitive to the camper who is trying to make contact with you. He may be in your own cabin, in your handcraft class, or in your swim class. He may stay behind to walk up from the beach with you. He may help you clean up in the craft shop. He will try to be where you are. He may be watching to see if you are a person he can trust with his deep feelings. He may make several attempts at discussing problems with you. He may use several testing techniques or try role playing. Your camper may ask, "Bill, what do you think of a guy who smokes pot daily?" He may not be tempted to try drugs himself, but may just be testing your reactions. Show patience and understanding, not alarm or condemnation.

Jane may stay around the cabin after the others have left. She is trying to make contact with you. Recognize this and leave the door open to talk, but do not pry. Be accessible when Jane is ready.

George may tell you that he has a friend who doesn't see anything wrong with cheating on an exam. What can he say to help his friend? George may be using this third-person approach to save face. He is afraid of what you would think of him if you knew that he had been cheating. Go along with George's third-person game. He may slip and change to the first person, but overlook it. Remember that your camper is thinking, *How much should I tell him?* and, *What will he think of me if he knows what I've been doing?*

Define the problem. Karen may test you with several surface problems until she trusts you enough to share the big problem that is bothering her. Don't attempt to give pat answers; there are no pat answers. Listen, listen, listen to *what* she says and to *how* she says it. Listen for what she omits. Listen for her feelings. What does she think about herself? Her parents? Her friends? Listen for distortions. Listen to what she selects to tell you. Listen for emotional overtones, a higher pitched voice, tears, or nervousness. She is telling you many things in addition to her words. The problem may seem trivial to you, but if it is big to her, it is big.

Your job is to listen, to reflect, and to clarify what she is saying. You may need to ask a few general questions to understand her feelings. She may say, "I have a sister two years younger than I," which may mean several different things. You can reflect her feeling by saying, "You are glad to have a sister near your own age," "You feel responsible for your sister," or "You resent being compared so often with your younger sister." Try to summarize what she has said. This is one way of helping Karen define her problem, so she can see it more objectively.

Remember that often just talking about a problem can be therapy. It's painful for some campers to put their feelings into words, but they often find great relief in just unloading to someone they can trust. Be careful not to probe, and stop them from telling you too much. They might regret it or feel guilty later on. Help remove emotional blocks so your campers can be more objective. Remember how Jesus did this when talking with the woman at the well.

Insight. Your job is not to solve the camper's problems but to help him gain insight so he can find the solutions to his problems. Do not just dish out advice; this is not counseling. Help your camper take responsibility for his problem.

At the point of insight, you may well introduce the Word of God. Direct him to read a passage or a verse which is relevant to his problem. Ask him what the passage means. Does he see any similarity to his problem? What might God be saying to him in this passage? Allow the camper to tell you.

Do not confuse him with many Scriptures, but help him understand the relationship of one or two. Take care not to be preachy. Resist saying, "Now if I were you . . . " Help him gain insight from the Word. Don't try to play God.

Remember that God loves your camper far more than you do, and in His sovereignty He places your camper in that broken home or in some other difficult situation. The Holy Spirit can give your camper insight and make him ready to change. Interject Scripture at points of readiness.

Timing is crucial. Beware of hurriedly giving him a verse of Scripture and telling him to pray about his problem before he has gained insight or understands the problem himself. But after the real problem has been exposed and defined, introduce a passage of Scripture that will help him. Let him see how this verse fits his situation. Guide him into seeing for himself a possible course of action, rather than telling him what to do.

Solutions. Help your camper discover one or several courses of action leading to a solution of his problem. Perhaps setting up a balance sheet of pros and cons will help him decide on the correct course of action.

POSSIBLE SOLUTION
GET A JOB AFTER SCHOOL

PRO	CON
Will have spending money	Grades may go down

Help him break down the solution into smaller steps. Though you try to guide him to right solutions, sometimes he may insist on trying a step that you do not think is best. Allow him the luxury of a minor mistake. Remember that counseling is a process of solving problems *with* people, not *for* them.

Follow-up. Keep in touch with your campers after camp.

Joe may be able to take some steps toward the solution of his problem while at camp. If he is not succeeding, you may guide him toward another course of action. Direct him again into the Word. Encourage him to believe that, with God's wisdom and power, he can solve his problems. He has the same access to God that you have. Keep in touch with him during the year. Encourage him. Show him how to feed on the Word and grow.

Help him establish a regular quiet time of prayer and Bible reading each day. Send him quiet-time helps throughout the year to encourage him to continue in this habit. Send him reading materials—tracts, books, or magazines that will be helpful to his Christian growth. Try to get him into a sound church where the Word is preached. Keep in touch with him through correspondence, round-robin letters, birthday and Christmas cards, camp photo exchanges, cabin reunions, and camp rallies. Try to get him into a Christian club or youth group. Enroll him in a Bible correspondence course if he is old enough. Keep encouraging him by answering his letters and circulating an after-camp newsletter. If you know of another Christian who lives near him, put him in contact with your camper. A mature Christian can help to disciple your babe in Christ.

Helpful Hints

Avoid saying, "When I had this same problem . . ." or your camper may feel that your solution must be his too. Perhaps it isn't.

Identify with your camper who has a problem, but do not become emotionally involved in it. Ask the Lord to help you show empathy and understanding, without losing the proper perspective.

Be shockproof. He may try to shock you with true or false stories of his escapades, to watch your reactions and see if you condemn him as a person. You can disagree with what he has done, but do not reject him. Jesus gave us an example of this when He spoke to the woman taken in adultery. He said,

"Neither do I condemn you," but He also added, "Go now and leave your life of sin" (John 8:11). He accepted her as a person, but rejected her sin.

Keep confidences. Resist the temptation to share some tidbit of confidential information, even to "get others to pray about it." What your camper has told you in confidence is not yours to share. Such information has a way of getting around, and your counseling ministry to that camper will end.

Don't jump to conclusions as soon as a camper begins to talk. Be careful not to treat his surface problem. Wait to get to the root of the real problem. (A Band-Aid doesn't help a broken heart.)

Recognize a deep emotional or psychological problem which may need professional help. Christian campers are subject to stresses and strains, as are non-Christian campers, and they may need more help than you can give them.

Give him your unhurried attention when he talks. Be a good listener. If you can't talk at the moment, tell him so and make an appointment for a later time, when you can spend time alone with him.

Don't try to cram a lot of information into him. Let him do most of the talking about his problem.

Show concern for his physical comfort. Don't keep him standing or sitting on a fence or window ledge. Make him comfortable and relaxed. The tension of his problem may make him perspire on a cold day, or it may make him feel chilled on a warm day.

Be interested in him without being nosy.

Don't try to solve your own problems through your campers.

Be friendly, outgoing. (If you aren't that kind of person naturally, you can be that kind of person supernaturally!)

Be careful not to identify with one side of a situation. Listen to all sides before passing judgment or trying to help a camper.

Be honest with your camper. He may ask, "Did my pastor tell you about me?" If you had a previous conversation with his pastor say, "Yes." But add that you find it hard to understand any problem secondhand and that you prefer to hear it from him. This shows that you are not prejudiced against him; the door is open for counseling, and you have been honest with him.

Be available to campers and approachable.

Your own example teaches much. Your campers want to see the Christian life demonstrated. Does it really work? Prove it to them by your radiant, enthusiastic walk with the Lord. Many campers' problems are rooted in the inconsistencies they see in adults' lives. Jimmy wants to see if you are genuine or phony. He is looking for reality in you. Will he find it?

By faith commit your campers to the Lord. Trust Him to work in their lives, to give insight, to motivate, to change. You might make a camper conform, but only the Holy Spirit can bring about the needed inner change. This is His work. Trust Him to work through you, to accomplish His purposes in your campers' lives.

6
Using the Word of God

What place should the Bible have in a Christian camp? How should we use the Word of God throughout the day?

God's Word is not merely a textbook referred to only in the Bible classes and other meetings. In a Christian camp the Word of God and biblical principles should set the framework for all activities. A spiritual emphasis should permeate camp.

The formal times of Bible study should not be isolated from the rest of camp. Since Christianity is "caught" as well as "taught," the demonstration of happy, wholesome Christian lives by counselors and campers helps make non-Christians want to know Christ in the same way.

There are some scheduled times for campers to learn from the Word of God. For example, in many camps a time is set aside at the beginning of each day, or right after breakfast, for campers to have their own quiet times.

Quiet Times

Camp is an ideal place to help campers form the habit of having their own quiet times. There is no practice more basic to a Christian's spiritual growth and maturity than the habit of feeding on the Word and finding answers to problems in the Word for himself. It is a thrilling experience for a camper to realize that the Lord can speak to him directly from His Word, without the help of a Sunday School teacher or counselor. If you can direct his dependence away from you, to God and His Word, you will help him establish a pattern of growth which may affect the rest of his life.

If quiet-time helps are provided by your camp, these may help guide campers' thoughts. You will find correlated quiet-time aids in some campers' manuals. If the idea of quiet time is new to some of your campers, give them special instruction in conducting one.

Some devotional guides provide questions to answer. Have your campers take along a notebook and pen to write down answers, and to jot down truths which the Lord reveals to them during the time they spend alone with Him. Such material might make for good cabin discussions later.

If no quiet-time materials are provided by your camp, try to direct your cabin group to Scripture passages which will meet their needs. Ask thought-provoking questions, or direct your campers to look for specific things in each passage, so that the reading will be meaningful to them.

There is much value in correlation. Reading for quiet time from the same book on which the Bible studies are based may help your campers discover and apply fresh truths to their lives.

Encourage each camper to find a quiet place alone to meet with his Lord. A log, a rock by the lake, a stump on a hillside may become a special meeting place with the Lord. Have him take along a sweater if it is cool, or a rain poncho to sit on if the ground is damp. He should have a Bible with clear, large-enough print. A reliable modern English translation, or a paraphrase such as *The Living Bible,* may help a camper better understand what he reads.

Your own attitude can help campers approach quiet time with expectancy. "What will God say to me today? What new thought will He reveal to me this morning?" Your Christian campers should expect God to speak to them. If they do, God will not disappoint them.

Quiet-Time Instructions for Your Campers

1. Begin with prayer, asking God to help you understand what you read today. Read the passage of Scripture out loud, if possible. Read slowly, thinking of each verse's meaning. Look for definite truths as you read the passage:

    Is there a sin that I should avoid?
    Is there a promise to claim?
    Is there a command to obey?
    Is there a blessing I ought to enjoy?
    Is there an example to follow?
    What can I learn about God?
    Is there a thought to take with me through the day?
    What can I learn about myself in this passage?

    Write the answers to these questions in your quiet-time book.
2. Think about what you are reading. How can you put this truth into practice today? How differently will you live today because you have read these verses? What difference will this make in your life when you leave camp? At home? At school?
3. Talk to the Lord about what you have read. Ask Him to help put His message into action. If there is a sin you need to confess, do so. If there is a command to obey, ask Him to help you to obey it today. Thank Him for what He has taught you about Himself. Thank Him for who He is. Worship Him this morning.
4. Plan how you will put these truths into practice in your life today.
5. Plan to share with someone what God has said to you this morning.

As a counselor, you are teaching by your example. Your own quiet time must be vital to you.

If you have young campers who cannot read well, you may have to go with them and read for them. Then let them answer the questions in your quiet-time helps. Be careful not to lecture. If you do not have written helps for your young campers, grade your questions to their understanding and needs.

If you have a camper who has never had a quiet time, go with him the first day and hold a quiet time with him. You may take turns having devotions with your campers. You can get to understand a camper better by sharing a morning quiet time with him. And it may provide you a rich counseling opportunity.

Bible Hours

In a conference type of a camp, or in a strongly centralized camp, Bible study is frequently taught by a platform speaker or Bible teacher. But if your camp is more counselor-centered than platform-centered, you will teach the Bible to your own cabin of campers. If you do, go over their general characteristics (pp. 44-49) again.

As you study each day's Bible lesson at camp, place before you the goals you have established for each camper. These will help you determine your aim as you teach this lesson. Reread the Scripture passage. Pick out the particular emphasis that will best meet the needs of *your* campers. Remember that your main object is not to cover Bible content, but to get your campers into the Word, in order that the Word may get into their lives.

Take time to motivate your campers. Decide on a lesson approach that will get them involved and thinking with you. If there is a clique in your cabin, you may set up a problem situation that is close to the real situation. They will see themselves in it. Make it just different enough that they will not resent it. Or you may begin with a true story about a camper their own age or an experience which you all shared together.

Use a newspaper clipping or an incident which recently happened in camp. Ask a thought-provoking question. "What do you think about . . . ?" In these ways you can get your campers thinking along with you.

Direct your campers to Scripture as their final authority

and let them have the joy of discovering spiritual truth for themselves. Refrain from saying, "This verse means. . . ." Direct them to a passage and let them tell you how it relates to the problem or the discussion at hand. Guide your campers into finding correct answers to life's problems in the Word. Ask them what difference this verse, passage, or lesson should make in the way they live. Make sure their answers are specific. Have them write down ways in which they can put a certain truth into practice. Allow the Holy Spirit to speak, for in the final analysis, application is His work. They may forget what you say, but they cannot forget what He says to them, particularly if they have dug it out for themselves. Provide opportunities to practice this truth at camp. Discuss at a later time how they were able to do this.

Methods of Study

You may want to study a certain portion of Scripture with your campers. To begin, have them read the entire passage in several translations. Ask the following questions. What is it about? Can you relate it in your own words? Does it have any new meaning? What precedes it? What follows it? Who were the original recipients of this message? Why was it written to them? How would you have received it had it been written to you at that time? Who was the human author? What do you know about him? What were the circumstances of his writings (e.g., Paul's letter to the Philippians about joy was written from a Roman prison)? What is the relationship of this paragraph to the whole?

If you are studying a book of the Bible, look also for natural divisions of the book. Apply the principle of proportion—how much of the book deals with one subject in relation to other subjects? For example, how many chapters or verses tell of the death and resurrection of Jesus?

Observe with your senses. Can your campers *feel* the rocking of the little fishing boat in the storm? Can they *smell* the costly ointment as Mary pours it on Jesus' feet? Can they *see* Lazarus coming out of the tomb wrapped in grave clothes, or can they *see* the fire coming down from heaven and lapping up the water and the sacrifice as Elijah prays? Can they *taste* the loaves and fish? Can they *hear* the priests of Baal shouting; can they *hear* the pigs squealing as Jesus sends the demons from the possessed man?

Use a Bible map; where did this story take place? Notice the time sequence. Look for contrasts and similarities. Notice figures of speech. Look up words in a Bible dictionary (some meanings have changed over the years). Notice the verbs. Are they active or passive? What tense are they? How many observations can you make from one verse of Scripture?

After *observation* comes *interpretation.* Do not try to interpret until you have thoroughly observed. Interpret in the light of context, historical background, semantics (word meanings), and the teachings of the entire Bible according to parallel passages.

Encourage your campers to take part in the lesson by varying your teaching methods. Use buzz sessions, debates, discussions. Divide your cabin group into research teams that will give reports on their findings. Have some of your campers serve on panels, conduct interviews, or serve as reporters.

Use imagination to make the Word come alive to campers. "How would you word the headline of the *Jerusalem Press* on that first Easter morning?" Have your campers write the Resurrection story as a feature article for the newspaper.

Spark the campers' creativity. "How would you design the cover for a paperback edition of 1 Peter? What colors would you use? What would be your layout?" Before your campers can answer, they will have to read the book to get its main theme.

Have campers write a play based on a passage of Scripture. For example, write the Book of Esther as a play and act out the drama of Haman and Mordecai.

Do a biographical study of a Bible character.

Make a comparison of Paul's letters.

Try to write a psalm about the outdoors as David did. Try

writing a stanza of a poem as in Psalm 119. Campers can gain a greater appreciation for the Psalms when they try to write one.

For younger campers the story method is always good. Tell a Bible story as if you had been there when it happened. Allow campers to act out a story. Use visuals aids. Use objects from nature—things growing on your campsite—to teach spiritual truths. Jesus taught lessons from a fish, a coin, a sparrow, lilies of the field, a fig tree, and a seed.

Try to reproduce the original setting if you can. If the weather permits, take your group outdoors for your Bible study. If is is cool, sit on blankets in a semicircle, or on some logs in a clearing in the woods. If your lesson is on John 21, study at the beach. Meet on a hillside for a lesson on the feeding of the 5,000, and in boats while studying Christ's teaching from a boat.

Above all, use variety. No method, no matter how good, should be used exclusively. Keep campers looking forward to Bible study with expectancy. Remember, teaching is not merely telling. You have taught only when campers have learned.

Campfires

In many camps, a campfire is the closing activity of a day or the week. This can be a most impressionable time for your campers.

If you are asked to speak at a campfire meeting, prepare a challenging message based on campers' needs and interests. This is not a time for Bible study or a long sermon.

Know what you are going to say well enough so you will not need to look at notes or use a flashlight. Stand to one side of the fire, so campers can see you and so you can see them. Watch their faces, their reactions.

Speak in a clear, loud voice. Do not raise your voice or shout, but speak distinctly and loud enough for all to hear. The group should be small enough so that an amplifier is unnecessary.

After the last song, begin immediatedly with your story or message. Eliminate introductions and preliminaries. You do not need to break the atmosphere of the songtime with a formal prayer before you begin to speak.

You may use a happening at camp as a springboard into your message. A reference to the day the sailboat capsized, or to the beautiful creek you discovered on an exploration hike will help keep your campers with you. You may call their attention to the sunset or to the call of a distant loon across the lake.

Some experienced campfire speakers believe that it's usually best to have only one point to your message. You may decide to use one Bible verse. Show campers how this verse points to God's Son, who wants to save them from their sins (or help them in some other area of their lives).

Perhaps you will choose to use the universally appealing story method at campfire. The story may be a Bible story told in the first person. Or it may be an event in the life of Christ, as told by an eyewitness. Or it may be a modern story which illustrates a Bible truth. It should be so vivid and so appropriate to the group that they get the application themselves. Do not ruin a story by tacking on a moral.

You may want to close with silent prayer or guided prayer. You may lead the group in silent prayer with a few words such as, "Thank Him now for dying for you . . . " "Tell Him that you love Him tonight . . . " or "Tell Him that He can use your hands and feet. . . ."

Singing a prayer chorus or a hymn may seal a decision. Perhaps a poem, or the words of a hymn spoken softly, will become the prayer of all.

Avoid playing on the emotions of campers at this time of day, when they are tired and have less emotional control, but do challenge them to action.

Long invitations may cause campers to come forward just to please you or some other adult. If younger campers have been sitting still for a long time, they may come forward because it gives them a chance to move. Be sensitive. You may want to ask campers to remain by the fire after the others have left. Do not pressure the group for decisions they may not understand or be ready to make. To go forward with no understanding or without a real pull from God may lead a camper into a false assurance and perhaps disillusionment later on.

Campfire can be a climactic time of day. Make it a time to remember, from the blazing fire, songs, and fellowship, to the last dying embers.

Cabin Devotions

Cabin devotions is a "family time" at the close of the day. The pace of camp has tapered off, and there's time for sharing together some of the day's thoughts.

Your campers should be all ready for bed before you begin. (If some campers are habitually late you may ask them to return to the cabin sooner.) Each camper will need his Bible and a flashlight, or you may want to use a lantern or candle lantern on the floor. You may use an electric light, but a bright, bare bulb isn't too conducive to the quiet atmosphere of cabin devotions. Keep the group sitting up, not lying on their beds. They may sit in a circle on the floor, or on several beds facing each other. (The circle formation says to each member, "You belong.")

If your counselor's manual does not provide correlated helps for nightly cabin devotions, you may want to read consecutively from Scripture or try to select passages on the basis of campers' needs. Discuss the passage together. This is not a time for preaching, but a time for spontaneous sharing. Be on the alert for any camper who monopolizes the discussion, or who uses this device to stay up later.

Fix an impression in campers' minds. Recall some lessons that were learned during quiet time, in Bible study, and from the campfire speaker. How do these lessons apply to life? Have questions been raised in their minds? How have your campers been able to apply the verse for the day?

Prayertime should be informal. Share requests for special

needs. Sentence prayers or conversational prayer may help all to take part. Do not force a camper to pray alone before he is ready. It may be during cabin devotions that he will pray for the first time. Discourage stereotyped praying and memorized clichés.

After devotions, lights go out and campers should be encouraged to go quietly to bed. No parties or roughhousing should follow devotions. The day should close with thoughts of the Lord in your campers' minds.

Missions

Many young people have the idea that missionaries are somehow superhuman, or far removed from the ordinary trials and temptations of life. The missionary at camp, whether he or she is a visitor or a counselor, can help campers realize that missionaries are real, ordinary people by getting involved in the daily activities of the camp.

Some camps take on a missionary project, such as a camp in another country. Letters, tapes, and pictures from the foreign camp are then shared with your campers, who share with the overseas camp. Think of all the fun your cabin could have, making a tape or arranging a series of slides that tell a story of your cabin, and sending them to campers in another land. Your tape may have to be translated, but this presents no problem. And music is the universal language, so the overseas campers will enjoy your camp singing.

International meals are fun. Food, facts, and costumes from different countries may make campers aware of missionary needs. Dining hall tables may be decorated to represent the countries where missionaries known to the campers are working. Or a progressive dinner might be conducted with foods characteristic of different countries served at various locations on the campsite. While campers eat, a counselor in the costume of each country tells something of the needs and work in that land.

You may include a missionary story hour in your program. Or an hour of cabin time once a week may be spent in making things for missionary children. If a missionary offering is taken, use it to buy something specific for the missionaries, something that the campers can see.

Avoid generalizations ("Bless the missionaries") in praying. Have campers pray for specific needs and for individual people. Let them know, if possible, when their prayers are answered. A missionary bulletin board with requests and pictures can stir up a lot of interest among the campers if it is changed frequently.

Interesting letters from missionaries, missionary children, or former camp staff on the mission field may be shared at mealtime. Each week the camp can concentrate on a different field. Flags and maps of those countries can be made and displayed, and interesting facts about the work in those countries posted on a bulletin board.

A missionary campfire can be a highlight event. True missionary stories can be told or pantomimed. They may be written by campers and presented at this special campfire.

Your camp might offer an advanced activity that stresses skills of outdoor living, such as woodsmanship or survival camping, and call the program junior missionary training. Many missionaries in remote areas learned to paddle a canoe, lay a fire, and lash a lean-to during their camping days.

Memorizing Scripture

Camp is an ideal place to learn Scripture because there are many opportunities at camp for campers to put into practice the verses memorized. You may have heard that the junior age is the golden age of memory, but too often juniors memorize without understanding. Their motivation for memorization may be an external award or reward, such as a plaque, pin, book, or even a week at camp. If the external motivation is removed, your campers may see no further reason to memorize Scripture. (Compare this with David's motive for memorizing, Psalm 119:11.)

Lead your campers in memorizing meaningful verses which they can use in their daily living at camp and at home.

Always use the verses they learn. Help campers claim the promises of God while still at camp. Jim may gain the courage to walk up the trail through the woods alone at night because he learned Psalm 56:3: "When I am afraid, I will put my trust in Thee" (NASB).

Reciting Psalm 91 together may carry your campers through the thunderstorm without panic, when lightning is crashing around their windblown tent on an overnight.

Susie may find courage to jump into deep water and pass her swimming test after learning Philippians 4:13: "I can do everything through Him who gives me strength."

Junior highs and senior highs can memorize too. In fact, they have more learning capacity than juniors, but they too must see a purpose for memorizing. They must be able to see how the Scripture relates to their present lives. You may have them memorize verses to use in witnessing, and then let them role play situations they may encounter in school.

They may memorize a psalm of worship for a Sunday morning service, and promises to claim to help them overcome temptation. They can easily memorize verses put to music. Campers may also commit to memory Scriptures arranged for a choral reading, and present the reading at a special camp service.

If memorized Scripture is to be learned, it must get into life. Memorization is not synonymous with learning; the proof of the learning is in the living. It is better to have your campers memorize one verse of Scripture and obey it than to memorize 50 verses and do none of them. Head knowledge without heart application is dangerous, for with knowledge comes responsibility. "Anyone, then, who knows the good he ought to do and doesn't do it, sins" (James 4:17). Your job is not to merely increase campers' knowledge of God's Word, but to help them apply the Word to their lives.

Leading Campers to Christ

Young campers want to please their counselors. When a public invitation is given to accept Christ, some may raise their hands at every meeting in order to please you. Others will "go forward" because their friends are going, or because they are tired of sitting still and crave movement. If a camper responds to an invitation, ask him *why* he came forward. Does he know that he has sinned? Does he understand that he deserves to be punished? Does he know who Jesus Christ is? Does he understand that Jesus Christ took his punishment in his place?

Do not overwhelm him with many Scriptures, but use one or two verses that he can understand. Avoid theological terms and the symbolism so often used with adults, which campers of junior age or under do not understand. "Letting Jesus into my heart" and being "born again" are symbolic terms that are not easy for young campers to grasp. One seven-year-old camper told his counselor, when asked to let Jesus come into his heart, "No, I would bleed to death."

A young mind thinks in concrete terms. He understands the difference between right and wrong and knows that doing wrong is sin. He can believe that he has sinned (Rom. 3:23). He can understand that wrong must be punished (Rom. 6:23). He can understand that Jesus Christ, God's sinless Son, took the punishment for his sins (John 3:16).

Let your camper pray, asking God to forgive him. Let him pray in his own words, thanking Jesus for taking his punishment on the cross (John 5:24). You may insert the camper's name in a verse of Scripture (such as John 3:16, 3:26, or 5:24). Explain any words in the verse that he may not understand. Have your camper tell you in his own words what he did and what Christ did for him.

Don't try to tell him everything you know about salvation at the time of his new birth. During the week, in quiet time, Bible study, and cabin devotions, you can help him grow in Christ. Also make it a point to spend some time alone with the new convert.

An older camper can more easily understand God's plan of salvation. He can realize his lost condition, and be willing to be saved from his sin through God-given faith (Eph. 2:8-9).

He can know who Christ is and what He has done for him. He can come into a personal relationship with Christ, an all-important step that many take at camp. Counsel with him as an individual, so that he understands clearly what he is doing. He may have raised his hand in a meeting when he was younger, yet never have had a genuine experience with Christ. If so, he may feel that he has tried Christianity, but it doesn't work. At this point he may be disillusioned or confused. It is your privilege and responsibility, as his counselor, to help him anchor his faith in Christ, the Saviour set forth in God's eternal Word.

Helping Campers Grow in the Lord

In a Christian camp, a spiritual emphasis should permeate each day. The Bible is not used only during formal times of Bible study, quiet time, and campfire. Nothing that a Christian does should be secular—all should be done for God's glory (1 Cor. 10:31).

"The heavens are telling of the glory of God, and the firmament is declaring the work of His hands" (Ps. 19:1, NASB) takes on new meaning while looking up at the clear, bright stars from a sleeping bag. And an hour in the craft shop becomes an opportunity to put Ecclesiastes 9:10a into practice: "Whatever your hand finds to do, do it with all your might."

Every activity in camp is an opportunity to live for Christ. For a new Christian, camp is an experiment in Christian living. Older Christians should learn to live increasingly more Christ-centered lives.

7
Planning Programs

The camp program is the vehicle for carrying out your camp's aims and objectives. All that happens to a camper, including the bus rides to and from camp, is the program. If your camp is centralized, it may have a closely scheduled program. A decentralized camp has a flexible program that is determined by campers' interests and needs. Whatever type of program your camp offers, there are a few basic factors to consider.

Factors Involved in Program Planning

Your camp's program should be planned to meet camper needs and to fulfill your *camp objectives.* How you do this depends on your camp *philosophy.* If one of your camp objectives is to help campers appreciate the outdoors, your program may provide opportunities for campers to sleep out under the stars, explore a stream, lay a nature trail, or sketch a distant mountain. If one objective of your camp is to provide a healthy place for campers to grow, but you let them buy as much candy as they want, or you do not provide enough sleeping time at night, you are not meeting a camp objective.

The *objectives of your campers* and those of their *parents* should also be considered. Remember that Sam comes to camp to have (1) fun and (2) adventure. Camp should provide fun and opportunities to do things he cannot do at home. Standard playground equipment, activities which duplicate the school yard, and craft kits which may be bought in a local hobby shop do not satisfy one's yen for adventure. If Sam's father sent him to camp to learn to swim, Sam should be put in a swimming class where instruction is given on his level.

If Mary's parents brought her to camp to learn to get along with others, camp ought to provide choice opportunities for Mary to interact with others in small groups—through cabin living, planning and working together on projects, and serving on committees with other campers.

The *sex of your campers* is also a factor in program planning. Girls are interested in some of the same activities as boys, but allow for their differences. For example, girls may choose to make jewelry and shell craft in the craft shop rather than making a knife sheath or boomerang. But both boys and girls will enjoy macramé and leather tooling. In sports, boys and girls should not compete against each other. In some activities they may work together; in others they play better by themselves.

The *backgrounds of your campers* and their *physical condition* are also factors. The *ages of your campers,* their *interests* and *abilities* should be considered. Fifteen-year-old Judy is not interested in doing the same thing as her nine-year-old sister Beth—at least not at the same time. Some graded activities (as riflery or swimming) may cross age differences, but even here an older non-swimmer appreciates being with those his own age and is often embarrassed to be placed in a beginners' class with someone six years his junior.

What *previous camping experience* have your campers had? Has Ricky been to camp every summer for five years? If so, he won't be interested in being led on a horse around a riding ring; he will want instruction in horsemanship. He will not be content with the same program he had in previous years, but will want something new and challenging. Activities with progression of skills will interest him. Some new activity offered for the first time, some skill reserved only for third- or fourth-year campers, some variety in programming will help Ricky enjoy his fifth summer at camp as much as his first.

How long is your camp period? Does camp run for one week? For two? Do some campers stay for a month or all summer? Your program should be planned to give one-weekers a sense of accomplishment and satisfaction, but should not be duplicated each week for the campers who stay longer. If you have several age-groups in camp—some new and some returning campers, some advanced and some nonskilled—programming is a complex job.

Perhaps you are thinking, *But I won't be involved in making the program.* You will probably lead some activities and assist in others. And there may be times when you along with your campers, will be planning a special event, a cabin time, or a stunt night.

Your own experience and skills are other factors that affect your participation in the camp program. The activities and classes offered should be limited to those that you and other staff members are qualified to lead. It's better not to offer an activity, such as riflery, unless a qualified instructor is available.

Your *campsite,* which may or may not have a lake to swim in, a mountain to climb, and a woodland to explore, will affect the program that is offered.

Your camp's *facilities* may limit or provide for your program. Are there canoes, sailboats, Ping-Pong tables, an archery range, backpacks for hiking? Perhaps there is a state park nearby, a forest preserve, an arboretum, a bird sanctuary, or a nature museum that is worth visiting. Your camp may have a pond teeming with living creatures, a woods full of rocks, trees, birds, wild flowers, and wildlife—all waiting to be discovered by your campers.

Keep in mind the *goals* you have set for your own group of campers when you plan that special cabin activity. An overnight may help you get close to Ted or break up that junior high girls' clique. A sound program hits individual campers where they live.

The factor of *budget* also affects program planning.

Expenses must be balanced by income, so you may not be able to have steaks for your cookout, or your cabin may not be able to have extra cake for a late snack. Campers can understand and accept such limits. But often a poor program is blamed on a low budget, when the fault really lies in poor planning or in wrong apportionment of funds. A fairly tight budget should not be an excuse for a poor program.

Sometimes a skeleton plan is made by the camp administration and the gaps are filled in by staff, counselors, and campers or committees of campers. In some camps the program staff, counselors, and campers work together democratically to develop the program. When campers have some say in the program, they become more enthusiastic and problems of discipline are greatly diminished.

How can you determine a good program for your cabin? Check each activity against the following test:

1. Does this activity contribute to the health of my campers? Is it fairly safe from physical danger?
2. Could this activity be done just as well or better in the campers' neighborhoods?
3. Do campers enjoy doing this activity? Is it fun for them? Would they want to do it if no points or awards were involved?
4. Does this activity increase the campers' understanding and appreciation of the out-of-doors?
5. Can my campers see the relevancy of God's Word to their attitudes and actions during this activity?
6. Does the activity help campers to be creative and resourceful? Does it help them think more independently?
7. Does this activity have carry-over value after camp?
8. Does this activity help my campers get along with others and develop a cooperative spirit?

A semidecentralized camp has certain hours for rising, going to bed, eating, resting after lunch, and perhaps for swimming. These activities, which affect the whole camp, are scheduled to avoid conflicts. The rest of the program is flexible in order to meet the changing needs and interests of campers. The program in these camps is by no means haphazard or unplanned, but takes much creative planning.

What different kinds of activities can be offered at camp? What are some less-common "camptivities"? How can you offer a variety of activities for the camper who stays all summer or returns each year?

Some activities can be graded into beginner, semi-skilled, and advanced classes. Try one new activity each week. One camp found that it could offer all of the following activities, with little additional expense and equipment:

Campcraft—introductory, intermediate, and advanced
Camping—trip, outpost, and survival
Sailing and advanced sailing
Hiking and advanced hiking
Conservation
Golf
Camp chorus
Drill teams
Star study
Bird study
First aid
Physical fitness
Fly-tying
Tin-can craft
Lashing projects
Archery—all levels
Riflery—all levels
Planetarium building
Building a tree house or a lean-to
Decoupage
Soccer
Swimming—all levels
Lifesaving
Water safety aide
Canoeing and advanced canoeing
Rowing and advanced rowing
Water-skiing
Gardening
Hockey
Camp orchestra
Camp marching band
Radio—shortwave sets
Tree study
Badminton
Ceramics
Copper enameling
Plastics
Metalcraft
Land animals
Insects
Map and compass—basic
Mapmaking
Oil painting
Nature crafts
Clay modeling
Volleyball
Candle making
Puppetry
Table tennis
Beadwork
Making camp equipment
Basketry
Skits and stunts
Group games
Team sports
Missionary projects
Camp newspaper
Leather carving and tooling
Papier-mâché
Jewelry making
Pond inhabitants
Flowers
Orienteering—advanced
Sketching
Water color landscapes
Basic arts and crafts
Photography club

Rock study
Home nursing
Angling
Weaving
Tilecraft
Seamanship and navigation
Air riflery
Obstacle course
Building an outpost campsite
Wire art
String pictures
Macrame
Horsemanship—all levels
Tennis
Wood carving—chip carving and whittling
Music appreciation
Tumbling
Individual sports: tetherball, handball, paddleball, fencing, etc.
Wrestling

Probably you can add to this list. All of these activities are not good for every camp, partly because of the lack of qualified leadership. Maybe photography is your hobby, or you love to draw or cartoon in your spare time. Why not interest your campers in this area? Small activity groups can afford your campers participation and interaction.

Typical Daily Schedules

Most likely your camp has a planned daily schedule. If so, you may post it on your cabin bulletin board. Know something about all of the activities, so you can interest your campers in them. A sample schedule might look like this:

Daily Schedule

7:00 Reveille
7:30 Flag raising
7:40 Quiet time
8:00 Breakfast
8:30 Cabin and camp cleanup
9:00 Bible study
10:15 First activity
11:30 Second activity
1:00 Dinner
1:45 Trading post
2:00 Rest hour
3:15 Third activity
4:30 Free swim
5:45 Supper
6:45 Evening program
9:15 Cabin call
9:40 Cabin devotions
10:10 Taps

Do not schedule too tightly. Allow 10 or 15 minutes to get from one activity to another, depending on the camp layout and the distance between activities. A camp schedule should not make campers feel they are always rushing about.

If your camp has more than one age-group present at a time and choices of activities are offered, the schedule could look like this one.

Daily schedule

7:30 Reveille
8:05 Flag raising
8:15 Quiet time
8:30 Breakfast
9:00 Cleanup
9:45 Bible study
10:30 First activity

Juniors	Junior High	High School
Beginner swim	Campcraft skills	Arts and crafts
Sports or games	Riflery	Nature
Archery	Canoeing	Sketching

11:40 Second activity

Juniors	Junior High	High School
Intermediate swim	Tripping	Intermediate and advanced swim
Campcraft	Crafts	Riflery
Hiking	Nature	Archery
	First aid	Canoeing

12:45 Lunch
1:15 Trading post
1:30 Rest hour
2:45 Third activity

Juniors	Junior High	High School
Arts and crafts	Beginner swim	Wilderness camping
Nature	Intermediate and advanced swim	Beginner swim
Music	Sports	Sports
	Sailing	Leadership skills
	Archery	

4:00 Free swim and craft shop
5:15 Cabin time
6:00 Dinner

Juniors	Junior High	High School
6:45 Evening program	7:00 Evening program	7:00 Evening program
7:45 Campfire	8:15 Campfire	8:15 Campfire
8:15 Cabin retreat	8:45 Cabin retreat	9:45 Cabin retreat
8:45 Cabin devotions	9:30 Taps	10:30 Taps
9:00 Taps		

Sunday Scheduling

Sunday should be a special day for your campers. It may be some campers' introduction to the real significance of the Lord's Day. Make it both a spiritually profitable and an enjoyable day, with a change of pace and a different or modified daily schedule.

Sunday can be a dress-up occasion, at least for part of the day. Sunday School may convene in small cabin groups, followed by a worship service in which the whole camp meets together in an outdoor chapel, weather permitting. Campers may decorate the "front" with wild flowers and pine sprays beforehand. Use camper choirs and ushers. Let a group of campers give the Scripture reading or let a speech choir read the Scripture. A special Sunday dinner, complete with dinner music and place mats or tablecloths, will make this meal a highlight. Recorded or live soft music in the dining room will help quiet an otherwise noisy mealtime.

What else can be done on a Sunday in camp? If campers arrive on a Saturday, and Sunday is their first full day of camp, programming is difficult, as the campers are restless, eager for action. It's not wise to try to keep them in meetings all day; nor in the opinions of most evangelical camp directors, should Sunday's program be just like every other day's. Most camp directors offer a modified program that is in keeping with their Christian convictions.

Many believe that Sunday is a good time to introduce the week's activities to new campers, to take a tour of the campsite and outpost locations, and to introduce camp traditions. Counselors often hold planning sessions with their campers, developing special evening programs or a cabin day program (a day when each cabin runs its own program).

A cabin walk, exploration, or hike is sometimes done on a Sunday afternoon.

Your cabin may want to discover its own secret hideout in the woods. Clear a fire site and then slip out to this special spot some night for evening devotions or a cabin campfire. Be sure not to tell anyone from another cabin where it is.

Selecting the week's activities may be done on Sunday afternoon, if your campers have a choice in what will transpire. Your cabin's crew may prepare for a supper cookout, or there may be a picnic supper for the whole camp. A progressive supper at different locations around the campsite, or a missionary progressive supper, can be a featured event. Here are some possible activities for a Sunday afternoon:

Read to your campers.
Tell a story.
Read or write poetry together.
Plan a worship or vesper service.
Write a missionary play.
Listen to good recorded music.
Sketch scenes around camp.
Write letters.
Role play situations they may face at home or in school.
Write letters to missionaries.
Write round-robin letters to campers who have left camp.
Make a cabin sign.
Decorate the cabin.
Make pins or cabin insignia for all cabin members to wear.
Play guessing games.
Take a photography walk, snapping pictures.
Make tapes of camp songs or tapes for missionaries.
Make a picture (or photo) story of camp.
Explore a pond or stream.
Conduct a quiz program.
Plan a cookout or overnight, including menus.
Make up a cabin song.
Hold debates.
Make scrapbooks.
Sing.
Conduct discussion groups.
Toast marshmallows.
Visit the nature nook and see what its program will be.
Visit the craft shop to see the display of crafts available and learn where the equipment is.
Learn the waterfront rules.
Practice knot-tying.
Bake a cake or make a pizza in a fireplace.
Go on a treasure hunt or scavenger hunt.
Cook supper out by cabins.

Your campers may be able to conduct a Sunday evening service in a nearby church. Many country churches appreciate it when campers conduct a service for them. Sunday afternoon may be spent preparing for this service.

If your campers stay in camp, the Sunday evening program should be special. Why not try a vesper service on the beach? Antiphonal singing from a high rocky ledge to a boat on the lake can set an atmosphere of worship.

The clear reflection of a floating campfire, lashed together and pushed out into the lake, helps campers remember a Sunday evening service long after the last embers die out. Or you may send out floating candles (one for each cabin) across the lake while a missionary message is given on the shore to your high schoolers.

Try telling your campfire message in the first person, as if you were an eyewitness to Jesus' miracles or as the boy in the crowd who gave Him his lunch (John 6).

If you are the campfire speaker, you may come toward the shore in a rowboat. Speak from the boat to the group gathered around the fire on the beach. Use a kerosene lamp, torches, or flares for light. If you tell Peter's life story in the first person, dress in a robe that Peter might have worn.

Conduct a trial according to present-day court procedures, letting campers tell what each of the following witnesses could testify about Jesus Christ. What might Mark have said if he were on a witness stand at Jesus' trial? Do the same with Peter, James, John, and other firsthand witnesses.

How would Mary have related the Resurrection story? Tell it as Mary might have done.

How would you have felt if you had been Moses when he saw that bush burning in the desert? What thoughts might have gone through his mind?

A missionary story, presentation, pantomime, or story acted out by campers is often an impressive Sunday night service.

There can be a hymn-sing in the lodge for older campers, after the younger ones have gone to bed. Counselors singing by lantern light in the cabin area after the campers are in bed can encourage quietness in the cabin after hours. If the camp bugler blows his calls on a trumpet or cornet, he may play a hymn after taps. This can put a final touch on a special Sunday in camp.

Evening Programs

As a rule, the evening program at camp should taper off gradually. Behavior problems at night are sometimes caused by exciting evening programs that leave campers at a high pitch just before they are expected to suddenly settle down for cabin devotions.

After-supper stunts, games, and special events should end before the campfire or wherever your evening message will be given. You may want to begin your time of singing with actions songs, rounds, and camp songs. You may shift from these semi-rowdy songs to choruses and hymns which will prepare your campers for the brief campfire or evening message. After a safari or scavenger hunt, campfire singing can serve as a transition from fun and hilarity to the more serious quiet part of the evening program. Your evening gathering should not be drawn out or play on the emotions of tired campers. It may run from 45 minutes to an hour in duration.

If the evening get-together is not at the campfire site, you may plan some transitional activity to get your group to your meeting place. If campers go on a treasure hunt, the treasure may be hidden near the chapel site. If you are using the campfire site, your last activity might be a circle game at this location.

Singing may take 15 minutes to a half hour or more, if interspersed with stunts. A verse or a short passage of Scripture, with a 10- to 20-minute present-day application, is usually long enough, for your campers' attention span at this late hour is short.

In general, campfire groups should be small. Meet by individual cabins some nights and with several cabins of one age-group on other nights. Many directors concur that it's best not to have more than one or two all-camp campfires a week.

The all-camp evening programs should be special events, such as the closing night, Sunday night, or maybe the first night of camp. These campfires might be made unusual by using a unique method of lighting the fire. It may be lit with chemicals ignited when a string is pulled, or by torchbearers or by torches carried by horseback riders, or by an Indian's flaming arrow after he comes across the lake in a canoe. Or a ball of fire can drop from a tree to light the fire (a cloth bag of sawdust, soaked in kerosene or fuel oil, may be lit by someone in the tree and slid down a wire that's stretched from the tree to your tinder).

Have your campers take along jackets, and perhaps blankets. Keep your cabin group together; sit with them, so that you can see their reactions to the message.

It may help to collect your campers' flashlights during the early singing: flashlights should not be allowed to become a distraction during campfire.

See that all campers sit fairly close to the campfire circle, not in little groups away from the fire. The campfire circle helps promote feelings of belonging and sharing each other's fellowship.

Prior to the campfire the evening program may include a *quiz program* such as "What's My Line?" "I've Got a Secret," or "Twenty Questions." Or there might be charades, stunts, skits, shadow plays, or a puppet presentation.

Amateur or *talent night* is a favorite of campers. Games, relays, contests of skill, or singing games may be held after supper and before the evening talk.

You might want to try a *gold rush*—finding pebbles painted with gold paint—or a pop-bottle hunt, a peanut hunt, or candy-bar hunt. These may be hidden in stumps, tied to tree branches, and tucked around cabins. If you are following an Indian theme, Indian games and contests, with campers and counselors dressed appropriately, and a ceremonial lighting of the fire will carry through the theme.

A *gypsy tournament* makes a good evening program, for which campers dress like gypsies. Small fires may be lighted around the central fire for each of the gypsy bands (cabins). Each gypsy band makes up its own song. Games might include hand-wrestling, leg-wrestling, and shoulder-shoving. Gypsy brew—cocoa or hot apple cider—can simmer over the fire.

For a change you might try a *candlelight and music*

banquet. Dessert may be cupcakes with a lighted candle on each.

The *story of Elijah and the Baal-worshipers* may be told or acted out around a campfire. A hidden narrator may tell or read the story from Scripture while the action of Baal's priests takes place around an unlit altar fire. Fire from a tree can be arranged to drop from above, to ignite Elijah's fire at the right time. A Bible story told this way is long remembered.

Candle ceremonies also contribute to an impressive campfire. Campers may walk to the campfire site carrying lighted candles, or the path to the campfire may be lighted by campers holding candles along the way. Or campers may be given candles at the close of the service. If the latter is done, the candles are carried down the path and extinguished before campers enter their cabins. A variation of this is to have each camper light a small twig from the last campfire. He blows it out, takes it home, and brings it back next summer, to light the first campfire.

A *closing campfire* can be impressive as campers put back into the fire until next year the blue of the lake, the green of the forest, the violet of the distant mountains, and the red of the sunset. Paper cups, with chemicals supplied by your druggist, can give these colors to the fire: potassium—violet; copper—green; strontium—red; cobalt—blue.

Flag Ceremony

Near the beginning of the day, usually before breakfast, most Christian camps take a few moments to pay respect to their country's flag. (At some camps the Christian flag, and occasionally other flags—state flags, camp flags, and even cabin flags—are also flown.) Before camp begins, learn proper flag etiquette and care.

A color guard helps make the ceremony impressive. These campers may be dressed alike, perhaps with clean white shirts and red sashes, or in a uniform. Color guard duty may be rotated among the campers.

Campers should stand at attention. Any uniformed personnel should salute; others put their right hands over their hearts. All should be able to see the flag being raised. A bugler playing "To the Colors," or a drummer playing a drumroll as the flag is being raised adds to the occasion's impressiveness.

After the salute to the flag a song may be sung. A Scripture verse for the day may be given at this time and prayer offered. The color guard remains at the flagpole until the ceremony is over.

The flag should be flown from sunrise to sunset. Many camps hold flag lowering ceremonies also. Hoist the flag briskly and lower it slowly.

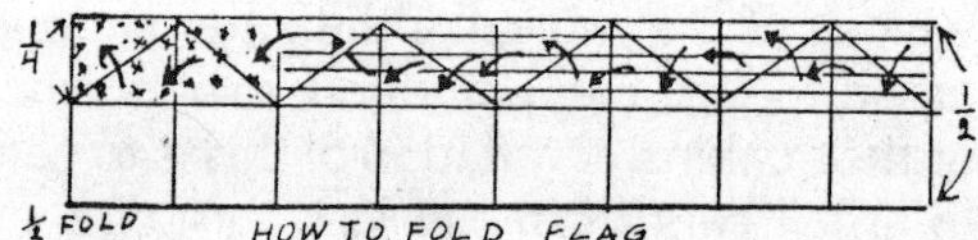

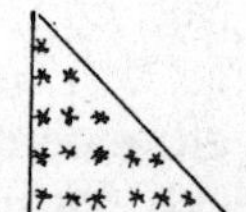

Mealtimes

Become familiar with your camp's mealtime procedures. Do campers enter the dining hall by cabins, or individually? At some camps the campers line up outside by cabins and enter the dining hall when all members are present. Do campers sit or stand while grace is being said? Is a table grace sung before this?

How is the food served? Is it done cafeteria style or family style? If family style, are there waiters or waitresses, or does someone from each table go and get the food? Does your camp have a rule about each camper tasting everything—at least a spoonful?

Mealtimes should be relaxed and enjoyed, with campers practicing good table manners. Tables should be set properly with dishes and silver arranged correctly, not simply piled at the end of a table. Strive to limit comments about food to positive remarks.

Is singing permitted while eating? Some campers neglect

to eat if there is too much excitement or noise. Some camp leaders save singing until the meal is completed and dishes are being cleared.

What is the procedure for serving food? For getting seconds? Does the counselor serve or are the dishes passed? With young campers usually the meat dish is served, but vegetable dishes are passed for campers to help themselves. Campers should learn to eat all of the food that they take.

How are the tables cleared? In some dining halls, dishes are scraped at the tables. At others they are even rinsed at the tables. In some places, tables are cleared and wiped by the campers. Do your campers do dishes? Or does your camp have a kitchen crew that does this? Do campers sweep the dining room floor after each meal? If so, there are schedules to be followed. If dishes are washed by campers, scrapers, racks, and sterilizer solutions should be provided. Laws in some states require that dishes be air dried, not towel dried. Music played while dishes are done, fancy hats for the dishwashers, special aprons or badges, or a special helping of food, make dishwashing fun rather than a chore. A counselor who works with his campers, whether they are doing dishes or peeling vegetables, makes it an enjoyable experience. Singing, exchanging riddles, and spinning yarns help make any chore delightful.

Rest Hour

Most camps provide an hour of relaxation during the heat of the day, after the noon meal. This change of pace, which is required by law in some states, provides needed rest for campers. Young campers may need more than an hour at times.

Campers may dislike rest hour because of its rigidity, or because they associate it with punishment or with the naps they used to take when younger. Since not everyone can sleep in the daytime, be flexible and try to make rest hour enjoyable. Let older campers write letters, being careful not to disturb a cabinmate who wants to sleep.

You could play soft recordings while campers are lying on their beds. Reading or telling a story while junior campers are lying down makes rest hour less of a drag.

If it is hot in the cabin, you may take your group outside. Take along blankets and spread them out under a tree. On a cooler day, when the warmth of the sun feels good, sunbathing may be enjoyed.

Sometimes campers may play quiet games or finish craft projects quietly for the first half hour and then spend the last half hour horizontally, with their eyes closed.

Take advantage of this hour for personal contact with your campers. Enjoy their company and let them enjoy yours. Above all, make this an enjoyable time, not an hour to be dreaded.

Free Time

A camp program should not be so closely scheduled that campers feel the pressure of always hurrying somewhere. As the American Camping Association states in its standards, "The pace, pressure, and intensity of the program should be regulated so that the campers will have time for leisure and can participate in [some] activities of their own will and at their own tempo."

To give campers time to relax, some free time should be scheduled, probably in the afternoon. During free time, sports equipment is available, the waterfront and craft shop are open, and the camper can do what he chooses.

Free time is even more important for campers who stay longer than a week or two. They may need time for personal things such as washing and ironing clothes, sewing on buttons, filing nails, and writing letters. They should have some time to putter, to climb a tree, to dream and think.

In some camps the hour before supper is called cabin time or tent time. On some days, this is additional free time for campers; on other days this time is used in doing things together as a cabin. Cabin time is used preparing for an evening program, getting ready for a cookout, decorating tables, or just relaxing. Your cabin may want to work on a project together. They may decide to build a raft, go canoeing, or—if the weather has been hot—take an extra swim (with lifeguards present, of course).

If campers have no unscheduled time, or if the tempo of camp is too fast, they become overtired and irritable; discipline problems arise. On the other hand, homesickness and discipline problems often result when campers have too much free time and too little supervision. It's up to your director to strike the happy medium.

8
Rainy Days and Other Fun Things

When Raindrops Keep Falling

What can you do with your cabin of campers if it rains all day? Well, tuck away in your camp duffel a supply of ideas for several rainy days, just in case.

After several busy days, a day of rain can be a welcome break in the tempo of camp. A camp committee for rainy-day plans may well be appointed, or the camp council may plan ahead for several rainy-day events. During cabin time on some clear day, you and your campers can lay plans for a rainy day. But don't let them carry out these plans until a day of hard rain. Soon they will be waiting for it to rain.

The book *Raindrops Keep Falling on My Tent* (Mackay, American Camping Association, 1982) is full of ideas on things to do with your cabin group or with the whole camp when the sunshine turns to liquid gray.

As much as possible follow the regular camp schedule, though you might want to let the campers sleep in. A hike in the rain can be fun if your campers dress properly and keep warm and dry with boots and raincoats. A rain hike or puddle hike after the rain provides an excellent opportunity to catch salamanders or examine spider webs that are glistening with raindrops.

An archery class can spend a rainy day repairing arrows and restringing bows. A sports class may conduct a sports clinic, playing indoors if the weather is too bad, or watching a film on skills or techniques. Free films on swimming, diving, and lifesaving are available from the American Red Cross. A swimming class may practice lifesaving procedures—indoors.

If it rains several days in a row, a special all-day surprise may lift campers' spirits. A circus, a county fair, a flower display, or an art exhibit can provide much creative fun, both in preparation and in execution.

If your camp has only one sizable indoor meeting place, careful plans must be made. Keep different games going on in the cabins and rotate the groups to and from the large building.

If it is a warm, slow rain and not a thunderstorm, swimming can be enjoyed. This may be some camper's first time to swim in the rain. Keep the swim period short and provide hot cocoa and a good rubdown when they come in. See that they put on dry clothes.

Don't forget the possibility of a wet-weather scavenger hunt. A rainy day may challenge older, more experienced campers' ability to keep dry in a lean-to, to build a fire (without paper, of course), and to prepare a meal outdoors.

The craft shop is always a busy place on a rainy day. If your craft staff offers a wide variety of projects, they may need your help on a rainy afternoon.

A photography class can continue, rain or shine. Composition, enlarging, cropping, and vignetting can all be done in the photography lab.

Costumes, games, puzzles, and other surprises can be kept in a special Rainy Day Chest. This should be kept locked and not opened till there is wet weather in camp.

Leaders from one camp brainstormed for rainy-day ideas. Here are some of their suggestions:

Run progressive games from cabin to cabin.

Play table games in the cabin.

Play charades.

Go on an indoor treasure hunt.
Conduct a scavenger hunt, in or out of the cabin.
Play indoor Ping-Pong (blowing balls).
Play round-robin Ping-Pong.
Play "magic" games.
Run off an indoor track meet.
Hold a Bible quiz.
Practice hair styling.
Make puppets.
Plan a skit.
Plan a cookout or overnight.
Sing and harmonize.
Have a special prayer meeting (perhaps conversational prayer).
Work on handcraft projects.
Figure out crossword and other puzzles.
Design an advertising poster of coming events.
Learn lashing and work on a project.
Try tumbling.
Work on tin-can craft.
Write letters.
Send round-robin letters to missionaries.
Get extra sleep.
Spin yarns (make up a story about your cabin).
Invent a cabin cheer.
Decorate a cabin.
Hold discussion groups and bull sessions.
Try indoor wrestling.
Exchange experiences ("My most embarrassing moment").
Practice campcraft skills (knot-tying, blanket rolls, trail signs).
Work on nature crafts.
Collate nature collections (leaves, twigs, bark, stones, wood, berries, cones, mosses, flowers, etc.).
Make a terrarium or aquarium.
Learn star constellations and stories about them.
Practice first aid and work out problems.
Practice lifesaving techniques.
Wash, iron, and mend clothes.
Write a song about camp or your cabin.
Read or write poetry.
Practice physical fitness skills.
Exchange riddles.
Put on wrestling matches.
Listen to recorded music.
Do stunts or skits.
Play mental games ("Who Am I?" "Twenty Questions").
Build a weather station.
Hike in the rain (look for insects, spider webs, etc.).
Collect worms for fishing.
Hold a sports clinic.
Sketch and draw.
Read good books or have someone read them aloud.
Make funny hats.
Make up a progressive story, each one adding to it.
Prepare a worship service.
Guess proverbs.
Act out situations that are described on folded sheets of paper.
Keep a cabin log.
Practice fire-building in the rain.
Make a fire board or knot board (samples for demonstration).
Undertake work projects (repairing equipment, clearing paths).
Hold an "indoor cookout" in the fireplace.
Learn the proper use of an ax and knife.

Put on a yo-yo tournament.
Conduct an indoor sports contest.
Hold a pie-eating contest.
Try bird study (identification or making models).
Practice orienteering.
Play map-and-compass games.
Practice mapmaking.
Work on fishing skills (fly-tying).
Do your cabin program-planning for upcoming days.
Polish all shoes in the cabin.
Have a hymn-sing.
Hold debates.
Put on a talent show.
Make a cabin sign or banner.
Learn Indian legends or the history of your camp area.
Make scrapbooks.
Make projects for missionaries.
Plan participation in a service at camp or in town.
Develop films and work on photography.
Role play situations campers may face when they go home.
Conduct a grooming session.
Have a Halloween, birthday, or other party.
Whittle.
Play indoor golf.
Plan a party or program with another cabin, or for a younger cabin.
Decorate the dining hall.
Decorate tables, following a theme.
Make costumes.
Dress up your counselor.
Make pins or insignia that all cabin members may wear.
Collect autographs and analyze handwriting.
Make a safety poster.
Pull taffy.
Bake cookies in the fireplace.
Have a panel on careers for Christians.
Do spatter painting.
Plant flowers in milk or egg cartons.
Put together a cabin or camp newspaper.

Rainy days are good for storytelling. If you can make up a story as you go along, all the better. Your campers may name items they want included in a story, such as a butterfly, a buried treasure, a horseshoe, a bone. As you spin the yarn, weave in these items. Such stories can be continued through several days of rain, and create their own suspense and anticipation in the hands of a skilled storyteller.

Does your camp have a library? Here is a fine place to foster good reading habits. There should be reference books and nature books in which your campers can look up what to feed the toad that Paul brought back from your puddle hike. If it has been a cold rainy day, prepare some hot cocoa for your evening program around the fireplace and the day will close with happy campers.

Music

A singing camp is a happy camp. Will your campers break out in spontaneous singing while hiking along a trail? Will they sometimes sing while playing a game? Will a chant or a round help make cabin cleanup time enjoyable?

In addition to hymns and Gospel songs, you may, at appropriate times, let your campers sing good fun songs and folk songs. Learn with your campers songs of the outdoors, such as "The Happy Wanderer" and "Land of the Silver Birch." Campers also enjoy some songs with their own camp name in them. Why not write a good one, and teach it to the entire camp?

Here are some songbooks that contain music suitable for camps: *Let's All Sing* (American Camping Association, Bradford Woods, Martinsville, Ind. 46151); *Joyful Singing* and *Tent and Trail Songs* (Cooperative Recreation Service, Delaware, Ohio 43015).

Be selective in choosing hymns, Gospel songs, and choruses. Help your campers appreciate good and godly words, and also cultivate a taste for quality in music. Choose songs which they can sing from their own experience, songs which are meaningful to them. Remember that young campers do not understand unexplained symbolism, as in "Jacob's Ladder" and "Give Me Oil in My Lamp." Before choosing a song you may ask yourself, "Have they experienced the truth of this song?" Avoid encouraging campers to sing about the joys of the Christian life if most of them do not know the Lord. However, all can sing songs that tell of the greatness of God and the person of Christ.

Most campers enjoy singing the solid hymns of the church. Singing "For the Beauty of the Earth" or "To God Be the Glory" can be a meaningful worship experience. "A Mighty Fortress Is Our God" appeals to active juniors. "What a Friend We Have in Jesus" can be sung with meaning by your junior highs, who sometimes feel that no one understands them. And don't forget the second stanza of "How Great Thou Art," which fits a camp setting so well:

When through the woods and forest glades I wander,
And hear the birds sing sweetly in the trees;
When I look down from lofty mountain grandeur,
And hear the brook and feel the gentle breeze;
Then sings my soul, my Saviour God to Thee
How great Thou art, how great Thou art!
Then sings my soul, my Saviour God to Thee
How great Thou art, how great Thou art!

Such music can help your campers worship, and can prepare them for Bible studies, campfire talks, and cabin devotions.

At campfire choose your songs carefully. After skits or games, campers are wound up. They are ready to sing rounds, camp songs, or fun songs. Perhaps you'll want to move from these to patriotic songs, then to the more quiet campfire songs, such as "Kum Ba Ya" and "Wayfaring Stranger." Tie your songs together with a short comment, unless the last line of one song leads naturally into the first line or chorus of another. Move smoothly from secular to sacred songs. Introduce meaningful choruses, and then hymns that gear into the theme of the message. Each song should further prepare campers for the campfire talk.

When you use music to prepare campers for a Bible study or message, don't ask them what they want to sing, for they don't know your theme. If you ask for favorites this tells them that you probably aren't prepared.

Impromptu singing around the piano, in the dining hall, and after meals is a fine time for favorites. The time while the dishes are being cleared away can be used in teaching new songs. Camp spirit can be molded by such group singing.

You do not need a piano or other accompaniment, for campers sing well without it. But if you play a portable musical instrument take it along to camp.

You do not have to be a trained musician to lead camp singing, though it helps if you can carry a tune and stay on pitch. You may use one hand to keep the rhythm and the other to control the volume. Show that you love to sing.

Many campers love to sing in choruses, trios, duets, and solos. And don't forget whistling and humming groups. Young campers who cannot sing parts can gain satisfaction from singing rounds and rhythm and action songs. Older campers love to sing descants and other songs around the fire which give them opportunity to harmonize.

Singing games are fun. Bible verses can be taught through song. Campers enjoy making up songs or parodies about their cabins, their leaders, and an overnight they have had. Use songs that fit your theme—your hymn of the week, or western songs for that Ranch Rodeo, or songs of the sea for your nautical theme. Some camps choose a theme Bible verse and hymn for their entire camp season.

A phonograph and a collection of good records in a camp library bring many hours of enjoyment to campers on rainy days. Expose campers to quality music and they will cultivate a taste for it. Books of the stories of hymns and composers give fresh insight into well-known hymns and songs.

After camp you'll remember the night your campers gathered on the rock by the lake, just before turning in for the night. The stars were so bright you saw them reflected in the lake's quiet water. Someone started singing "Fairest Lord Jesus."

> Fair is the sunshine,
> Fairer still the moonlight,
> And all the twinkling starry host
> Jesus shines brighter,
> Jesus shines purer,
> Than all the angels heaven can boast.
> . . . None can be nearer, fairer, or dearer
> Than Thou, my Saviour, art to me.

There, in the quietness and stillness, you and your campers worshiped. This is one contribution of music to camp.

Storytelling

A good storyteller never lacks an audience. A story can teach, relieve tension, develop imagination and creativity, and motivate to action. You can prepare your group for camp experiences through stories and you can interpret experiences to them through this same method.

Prior to camp, practice telling stories to your family, to younger brothers and sisters, to neighborhood youngsters. Know what you are going to say and the emphasis you wish to make. Have the logical sequence of events clearly in mind. Make brief notes, if you want to be sure of yourself. Do not memorize the whole story, but you may write out your opening sentence. Your story should have a plausible plot and should conclude with no loose ends.

Begin with action. Christ did this: "A farmer went out to sow his seed" (Matt. 13:3); "A man was going down from Jerusalem to Jericho" (Luke 10:30). Plunge right into your story. Get your listeners involved right away.

Here's a general list of storytelling tips:

Avoid long introductions and long descriptions.

Be careful not to give your whole plot away in your introduction. (*Example*: "Now I am going to tell you about a boy who put his finger in a dike and stopped a leak and saved his country.") This spoils the story's surprise element and campers' interest.

Use direct discourse whenever possible.

Change your voice for different parts.

Tell action stories that relate to your campers' interests and the world around them.

If you are making up a story, you'll do well to make your characters boys and girls the ages of your campers.

Before telling a story, visualize its characters. Feel as they did. Put yourself in their places.

Look at your campers while you tell the story.

Do not use meaningless gestures that distract from your story, but appropriate gestures which make the story more vivid.

Practice telling your story in front of a mirror and taping it on a cassette recorder.

Don't try to tack on a moral at the end. If your campers haven't gotten the point without this, you have failed.

Speak in a clear, natural voice. Speak fast when the action is fast, and slowly if "Jimmy is creeping slowly up the stairs." Whisper when "He is tiptoeing into the bedroom. . . . "

Use your imagination as you tell the story. See it. Live it.

Use active rather than passive verbs.

Describe your characters by comparison, by gesture, and by action so that your campers may visualize them too.

Juniors can comprehend time and place. They like to know where your story takes place. Associate the time with some event they already know. "While George Washington was president, a man who lived in Philadelphia . . . " or "The distance from Jerusalem to Bethany is about as far as from our dining hall to Lookout Point." This orients your campers, so they can better understand the action that is about to take place.

Juniors like hero stories with action and suspense. At junior high age the heroes must be realistic. High schoolers like stories of how people succeeded and how people sacrificed for what they believed in. They like realistic situations, some idealistic stories, and stories of other teenagers. Lives of missionaries make good story material.

When telling Bible stories, make the characters real to your campers. You may have to clarify some words so they can understand certain incidents. Be true to the facts of Scripture, but make the story come alive. You may tell the story in the first person as an eyewitness account. Or you may tell a similar story in a contemporary setting. This technique leads campers to recall the parallel Bible story and helps them relate its spiritual truth to their lives.

Special Days

Special days add variety to your program and involve campers in exciting preparations. Ignoring the calendar, you may celebrate any holiday on any day. If you pick the *Fourth of July,* line up a parade or a patriotic pageant.

Why not celebrate *Easter* with an early morning Easter sunrise service on a hillside or mountainside? An Easter parade of camp-made hats may be added later in the day.

Valentine's Day, May Day, with a maypole, and *Thanksgiving*—complete with a turkey dinner and Thanksgiving service—make successful special days.

A *Christmas* celebration is always special in camp. Campers decorate their cabins, hang up stockings (filled by counselors), exchange names within their cabins, and make gifts in the craft shop for their cabinmates. A Christmas tree can be decorated with paper chains, whipped detergent snow, pine cones, and popcorn balls. Campers like to make these decorations and trim the tree. The music for the day will be carols. (Counselors or older campers go caroling by lantern light the night before.)

Why not try a *Sadie Hawkins Day,* a *Winnie-the-Pooh Day,* a *Pirate Day,* a *Hobo Day,* an *Indian Day,* or a *Western Ranch Day* with an outdoor barbecue and rodeo? Days which feature various countries, such as *Mexican Day, Netherlands Day, Swiss Day,* and *Japanese Day* include decorations, costumes, and customs of these countries, plus special programs. On *Japanese Day* older campers may leave their shoes at the door, try to eat with chopsticks they have made, and sit on the floor while eating from low tables.

A *Circus Day* or *County Fair Day* takes many hours of preparation by your campers. Each cabin may enter an exhibit at the fair (e.g., largest orange—a volleyball covered with orange paper).

Or you may concoct a *circus sideshow.* Tents can be made from blankets and sheets. Imaginative campers will be able to devise such entries as the thin man, the giant (camper standing on a chair behind a blanket), the Siamese twins (two campers in a large sweat shirt, probably yours), or a magician act.

Try an *Olympic Day,* with sports events. You can even have a runner with a torch start off the day's schedule.

A *Paul Bunyan Day* can include a wood-chopping contest, tall tales, and a roast-pig barbecue.

An *all-camp birthday party* can celebrate everyone's birthday. Twelve tables may be decorated for different months of the year. Campers sit at the tables of their birthdates. Cakes and candles are included. Try making up some original birthday songs!

For an exciting change of program, you might try a *Camper-Counselor Day.* A camper in each cabin is chosen to be the counselor for the day. You then take that camper's place for the day. Other campers are chosen for the jobs of unit leaders, camp director, and the administrative staff. Campers often mimic the leader whose place they are taking. You'll be surprised to see yourself as your campers see you! And the counselors, who are campers for the day, often give the campers a taste of their own medicine. (You are not really relieved of responsibility. Camper lifeguards, for example, must sit beside the real lifeguards during the swim period.) The camper-nurse for the day spends time helping the real nurse in the infirmary. It is not only a hilarious day, but campers learn a little responsibility and better understand their leaders' jobs.

Girls go for *Color Day, Plaid Day,* or *Stripe Day.* This means that every camper must wear something of that color, plaid, or stripe in order to get into the dining hall.

On a *Backward Day* the daily schedule is reversed, with supper in the morning and breakfast at night. Clothing is worn backward and grace is said at the end of the meal.

Be creative and you can add many more ideas to this list. Keep a daily log of programs and you will have a wealth of ideas for future years. Note the programs that went well and those that need revision.

Special Events

Try a *track meet.* This can be held outdoors—or indoors on a rainy day (with paper plates for the discus throw, Ping-Pong balls for the shot put, straws for the javelin toss, etc.).

A *tug-of-war* is fun in shallow water or across a small stream. Someone is bound to get wet.

A *nature exhibition* can be held with blue ribbons going to the largest flower, the smallest or largest leaf, the most shells, or some other classification.

Photography displays or *clothesline art exhibits* may help an unathletic camper achieve recognition.

Tests of campcraft skill are interesting. Each camper can choose one 12-inch log. He will have to chip this for kindling and tinder. No other fuel or tinder is allowed. The object is to build a fire with 3 matches and boil water in a No. 10 tin can. A variation of this involves tying a piece of string between two trees, about 18-24 inches above the ground. Campers build fires under the string, to see who can burn the string first.

A *political rally*, with a platform and mock campaigning, can be fun.

A *moonlight hike* or *night hike* can acquaint your campers with night sounds. Do not force campers to go, but usually this is an event to which they look forward.

A *water pageant* or *synchronized swimming* can be colorful and beautiful. A water carnival can include races and contests for landlubbers, beginners, and advanced swimmers. (Get the book *Water Fun for Everyone*, Association Press, 291 Broadway, New York, N.Y. 10007.) Boating and canoe racing, stunts, and demonstrations can be included.

Campers enjoy *camper-counselor activities* when the staff plays with handicaps. For example, in baseball, counselors must run backward to the bases, or run to bases carrying a pail of water or pushing a wheelbarrow.

An *arts and crafts show* can display articles made by campers during the week.

A *horse show* can demonstrate riding ability. A variation of musical chairs may be played on horseback. Polo and relay races add to the excitement.

An early morning *sunrise hike* can be an unforgettable experience. Many city campers have never watched a sunrise, so some morning take your cabin group to a nearby hill or clearing to watch the sun come up. Sit quietly, watch, and listen to a day being born. Perhaps the reading of a poem, like "Sunrise" by Edgar Guest, will enrich your campers' appreciation of the sunrise. The singing of a hymn or the reading of Psalm 8 will make this a memorable morning.

Sometime try a *lantern party*, a *torchlight parade*, or a *hayride on a farmer's horse-drawn wagon.*

A *carnival* with beanbag throws, fish ponds, ring toss, peanuts, popcorn, and maybe even cotton candy adds variety. An outdoor supper may be served on Carnival Day with Kool-Aid at one booth, hot dogs at another, and ice cream bars or other courses at other booths.

Try an *amateur night* or *skit night,* with campers making up original skits. Plan a *music concert* with campers and staff participating.

A *deaf-and-dumb meal* or a *one-utensil meal* gives variety at mealtime. During a deaf-and-dumb meal no one can speak. For the one-utensil meal dump forks and spoons in a big box by the door. As campers enter, they draw out a single utensil, with which they must eat their whole meal. Counselors are usually given special kitchen utensils such as soup ladles, spatulas, and potato mashers. (Maybe you'll hope that a camper doesn't take your picture to send home to his parents.)

Ever try a *counselor hunt?* During supper the counselors slip out of the dining hall one at a time, unnoticed. Each hides somewhere around camp. At the close of the meal, someone announces that the counselors are missing and the campers must find them. They may be hiding in trees, on roofs, in caves, under buildings, etc. Boundaries are described and some places may be made off limits.

A *stuffed animal* or *pet show* can be held. Blue ribbons may be awarded to the biggest, the smallest, the best-dressed,

and the most original pet. Campers may either make or collect their own pets.

Work Projects

A work project, or service project, is an investment of energy that can be a satisfying experience and give campers a sense of fulfillment. There is satisfaction in hard, physical work; there is pride in accomplishment, in a job well done. Camp is more "theirs" after campers have helped improve it.

After a camper has paid his camp fee, some leaders are afraid to suggest that he help clear away brush, plant trees, or clear trails. But young people, properly led, like to make a contribution and leave a part of themselves at camp. Campers can learn some good work habits, skill with tools, and how to work cooperatively with others. Campers and counselors get to know each other better while working side by side.

Building a tree house or a lean-to or developing an outpost campsite can help Harry become a responsible member of your cabin. If he feels that his job is important he will try his best. It may be building a cage for a baby animal, or a food box for trips out of camp.

A group of campers from one camp spends a day of their canoe trip with a forest ranger, helping clean up campsites, blazing trails, or whatever the ranger suggests. This day of service enriches the whole trip. And what good public relations it is for that Christian camp!

Perhaps your cabin will decide to caulk and paint the rowboats, build outdoor rustic benches, or repaint furniture. You can be sure that they will take pride in their project and instruct others to take proper care of it. An outdoor barbecue built by high school boys may be enjoyed by the whole camp. Bulletin boards, a sundial, steps up a hill, or a log bridge over a swampy area can benefit both camp and campers.

Rather than assign service projects, let your campers choose their own. Be sure to check with the administration for approval before the planning goes too far. Have enough good-quality tools available and a budget to cover any supplies you will need. Give recognition when projects are completed. A special party may be given at the new overnight spot, or a banquet held for your cabin when they complete their nature trail.

9
Friends, Foes, and Fun

Nature Program

Did you ever feel the furry branches of a staghorn sumac, or notice the square stems of a blue ash? Did you ever find an owl pellet and see what Mr. Owl had eaten recently? He keeps down the mouse and shrew population after dark.

Ever taste the red (not white) berries of the sumac? What do they taste like? Ever boil the bark of a sassafras root?

Did you ever make a plaster mold of deer tracks? Did you ever make colorful place mats with dyes made from berries, or drinking cups from birch bark, or press leaves between waxed paper with a warm iron? Did your senior high girls ever discover during their four-day canoe trip that the cones of the white pine make good hair rollers?

Nature should be a part of each camper's daily experience. You can help your campers learn about God's creation in its natural setting. Twenty-five dead insects mounted on a board and identified with Latin names hold little appeal to campers. But your group may sit quietly on a log to watch an ant dragging something many times its size. They will enjoy hiding quietly in a thicket to watch a black-masked raccoon steal the garbage you put out for him.

Observe animals in their natural habitat rather than in

cages. If you keep animals for observation, keep them only a few days. Some animals that are kept captive all summer cannot forage for themselves when winter comes.

Spend some time in the nature nook before your campers come. Know something about the nature program your camp offers.

Learn to identify some star constellations. Be able to show your campers how to find the North Star, the Northern Cross, the Ice Cream Cone (Boötes), the Dragon, and the Crown. On an overnight learn to tell the time by the position of the Big Dipper in the sky.

Help your campers feel at home outdoors at night by being able to identify night sounds. Sit on your cabin steps some night with your campers and see how many sounds you can identify. Do you hear loons on the lake or the hoot of a distant owl? Can you recognize the sound of the wind in the pines or the noise made by branches rubbing on your cabin roof?

At camp Jim and Betty will meet living things all around them. As a counselor you help interpret their experiences. To a camper not accustomed to the woods at night, the soft footsteps of a friendly chipmunk may be like those of a lion or tiger. Help him recognize sounds and he will not fear them.

To be a nature counselor (and every counselor should make a stab at it) you don't have to be a biology major or be able to identify or know technical names and facts. But you should possess curiosity, enthusiasm, and a sense of wonder. Be able to open the door of God's revelation in nature to your campers' inquisitive eyes.

Be willing to stop, to listen, to look at all the growing, living things around you. When Bill brings a newt and stumps you by asking, "What does it eat?" be honest and answer, "I don't know." But also add, "Let's watch it and see if we can find out." It takes time to watch a mother bird feed her young, explore a pond, or follow a snail's silver track. But take the time to observe the care God has taken with little things—the perfection of a tiny wild flower, the wings of a dragonfly.

Then on a starry night lie on your back, look up, and

wonder at the vastness of God's huge universe. Let your campers worship with the words of Psalm 8: "When I consider Thy heavens, the work of Thy fingers, the moon and the stars, which Thou hast ordained; what is man that Thou dost take thought of him?" (v. 3, NASB)

There is so much to observe around camp—creeping crawling things, buzzing flying things, chirping singing things—the crickets, toads, salamanders, grasshoppers, tadpoles, turtles, frogs, snakes, fish, ants, caterpillars, birds, chipmunks, mice, squirrels, skunks, raccoons, and on and on. Are snakes really slimy? Touch one (a nonpoisonous one, of course) and see. Do toads give warts? Pick one up. How does a tree toad make a noise? What does a field mouse eat? How does a cricket make that chirping sound? Nature study can open a whole new door to excitement and adventure and give your campers a greater understanding of the Creator who "richly provides us with everything for our enjoyment" (1 Tim. 6:17).

Have some nature sourcebooks available for your campers. Some good ones are the inexpensive Golden Book series on rocks, birds, trees, flowers, weather, fish, mammals, reptiles, and amphibians as well as the series of Golden Books on *Nature Crafts* and *Wild Animal Pets.* If you don't know all the answers to Pete's questions, it's good to know where to direct him to find the answers. (See the Bibliography for other sources.)

Bulletin boards with nature quizzes (matching leaf with bark, or cone with needles) and objects which are changed each day create an interest among campers.

A *what's-it box,* with a protruding shirt sleeve into which campers put their hands and identify objects by feel, teaches via the sense of touch.

Electrical quiz boards where birds, wild flowers, etc. are identified, are irresistible to campers if located in the heavily trafficked areas of camp—by the mailboxes or just outside the dining hall. When a camper identifies a bird or object correctly, a bell rings or a flower lights.

Peep-boxes that say, "Don't look!" or "Beware!" intrigue campers and arouse their curiosity.

The camp's *nature museum* may be in a corner of a lodge or just out under a tree. Maps, weather predictions, and samples of leaves or twigs may be displayed. Be careful not to pick flowers that are scarce. Leave them for others to enjoy.

The *nature nook* can be another fascinating place for campers. Here reference materials, supplies, and tools should be kept. These may include binoculars, magnifying glasses, spatter paints, nets, a killing jar, a small cage or two (for transient guests only), jars, tin cans, plaster of paris, and perhaps blueprint paper for leaf- or fern-prints. A small microscope is helpful but not necessary. Bird records (the actual bird calls recorded by the Laboratory of Ornithology at Cornell University, Ithaca, N.Y.) will be helpful (and useful on a rainy day).

Marking a *nature trail* is an exciting as well as educational experience for campers. The trail should be within easy access and should be in a natural area through meadow, woods, and around a stream or pond. Keep the trail narrow. Mark objects so that campers will be led into discussion or research. A question such as, "Who lives here?" is far more interest-grabbing than "Barn Swallow's Nest." To help your campers observe more closely, give them cards to fill in as they walk along. Wooden markers, painted tin-can lids, and varnished tags make satisfactory markers.

Luminous paint may be used to mark the trail after dark. Campers may view star constellations through tin-can tubes that are fastened to stumps and swiveled. A chart may indicate the locations of constellations at different hours.

It's good to change the trail during the summer, to include more of the changing wildlife.

Bird study is one of the most popular branches of nature study at camp. Bird walks are best in the early morning or late afternoon. Watch a bird family. Who sits on the nest? Do both mother and father share in feeding their brood? Listen to a bird's call, song, and chirp. Can you tell when he uses each?

Old abandoned nests may be collected. Bird models may be constructed in life sizes and colors. Bird eggs can be made of plaster and placed in the proper nests.

Look at a bird's bill through field glasses. Is it short and thick for cracking seeds? Is it pointed and long for drilling into bark for grubs? Look at his legs. Do his long spindly legs tell you he wades in water? Or are his toes arranged for perching on branches? What is his flying form? Is it long and gliding, or does he make short and jerky movements? What is his color? Does he have wing bars? What is the shape of his tail feathers? Keep a bird census of what birds are seen, when, where, and by whom.

Why not set up a *weather station* at camp? Campers can make predictions each day. Homemade equipment will do. Weather maps can be ordered for the camp.

A most important lesson is learning to take care of God's creation and showing respect for other living things.

Terrariums, aquariums, a *fernery,* a *cactus garden, dioramas,* and an *ant colony* can relate nature to your craft program.

Fishing can be great fun at camp. Make your own poles, lures, and lines. Help your campers recognize the various kinds of fish in your area. Try mounting a good specimen. Or clean and cook a fish your campers have just caught.

Put some food out to attract *small animals* and see how tame they become when you do not frighten them. Watch for animal tracks in the soft mud or on your beach. How many can you identify? See if you can figure out what Sammy Squirrel was doing. Why did he stop here? Was he running? Did he bury something here? What did he bury? Where did he go next?

Trees are all around us at camp. How many different kinds are there at your camp? Can you identify them by color, leaf, bark, flower, bud, seed, and shape? Which ones are shaped like upside-down ice cream cones? Which look like lollipops? Why do poplar leaves constantly tremble in the breeze? To see why, examine their leaf stems.

Count the rings on a fresh stump. How old was this tree? Can you determine the rainfall during some past summers by the growth rings? How thick was this tree when most of your campers were born? How thick was this tree when World War II began? Let your campers mark several historical dates with small flags.

Study the *geology* of your camp. What rocks or minerals are to be found on the site? How did they get there? Which rocks are good for a fireplace? Which should *not* be used to cook on? Is there a spot at camp where you can see layered rocks? A pothole by the side of a stream? A fault?

What *plants* are native to your area? What wild flowers? How can you recognize the mint family? Have you ever tasted mint leaves?

What berries are edible? What plants are edible? (Be sure you know before you eat.)

What plants did the Indians use for dyes? Put some Indian dye on your hand.

Did you ever look at soldier moss under a microscope?

Could your campers collect wild flower seeds and plant a garden in an egg carton?

The distance you cover on a nature walk is not important, but what you find along the way is. Turn up old logs, move rocks, poke into holes, dig into mud, wade into streams, open nuts, eat wild raspberries, smell the odor of bugbane, lie on your back and watch the clouds drift by. A nature walk is an experience for the senses. Your campers can learn to appreciate nature. They can learn to listen, to explore, to climb, to wade, to sing, to walk, to feel, to watch, and to be quiet and see

God's revelation of Himself in His creation.

Camp Pests

Can you identify *poison ivy, poison sumac,* and *poison oak* if they are growing on your campsite? Mark poison plants along your nature trail with a skull and crossbones, so that campers may recognize and avoid them.

Ivy may grow along a path or fence, or it may grow as a vine up the trunk of a tree. Though poison ivy has three shiny green leaves and turns to a beautiful orange with clusters of white berries in autumn, you won't want to use it for decorations. Do not burn it or let it get mixed in your firewood.

Poison sumac should not be confused with the harmless staghorn sumac which has red berry-like tassels, fuzzy branches, and toothed leaves. Poison sumac has smooth branches, smooth-edged leaves, white hanging berries, and grows in marshy ground. Both staghorn and poison sumac turn brilliant colors in the fall.

Poison oak is not an oak but has three shiny leaves that resemble oak leaves. It is found mostly west of the Rockies, and grows as a shrub.

After contact with any of these, wash contaminated areas of skin or clothing with soap and water. Consult your camp nurse if symptoms of poisoning (itching, blisters, swelling, skin eruptions) appear. Avoid scratching—this can cause spreading and infection.

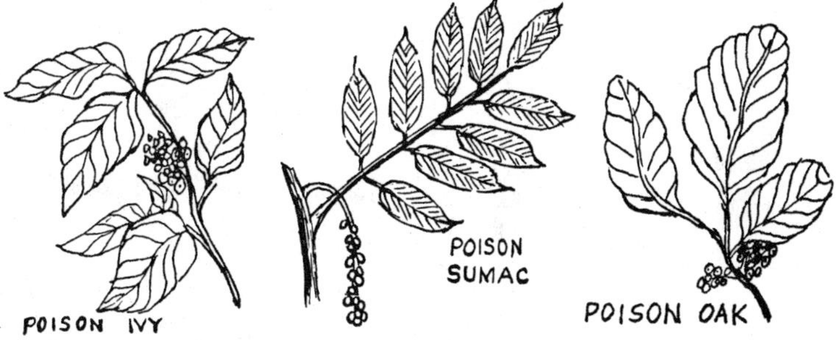

Girls probably dislike *snakes* more than any other creature around camp, though only four kinds of snakes that live in the United States are poisonous. Snakes do not chase people. They do not roll in hoops; they do not leap at you; they have no stingers in their tails or tongues. (Their tongues are actually sensitive antennae.) Most snakes eat mice and smaller pests and are helpful to man. Teach your campers not to kill every snake they see. A snake is more afraid of you than you are of it and wants to be left alone. Unless you frighten or harm it, it will be glad to run away from you. Snakes are perfectly dry to the touch, but they feel cool because they are cold blooded.

The poisonous snakes in the United States are the coral, the rattlesnake, the copperhead, and the cottonmouth.

The *coral snake,* found in the South and Southwest, has bright red, yellow, and black bands. It is often confused with the harmless scarlet king snake, which has red, black, and yellow bands. A good way to remember which is which: "Red and yellow, kill the fellow." If the red and yellow colors are next to each other, the snake is a poisonous variety.

The *rattlesnake* is so called because of the horny rings on its tail which make a buzzing noise when vibrated.

The *copperhead snake* is found in the eastern United States and is recognized by its copper color and its triangular head.

The *cottonmouth,* also called the *water moccasin,* usually

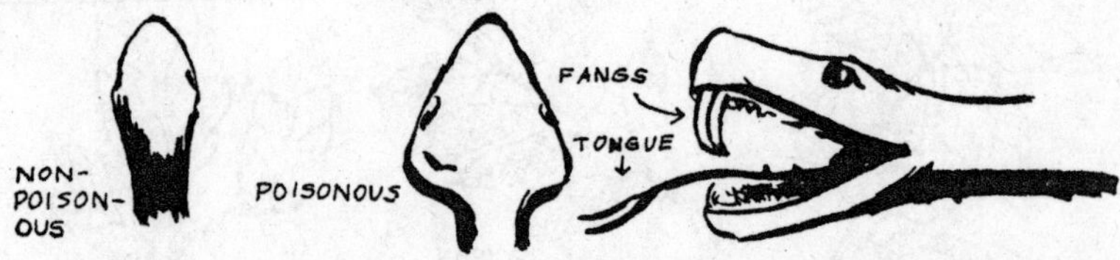

found in swampy areas of the South, is olive brown in color and gets its name from the white interior of its mouth, which it frequently opens when about to strike.

All poisonous snakes except the coral have triangular shaped heads and elliptical eyes. (Harmless snakes have oval-shaped heads and round pupils.) A poisonous snake's venom is released through its fangs, which are two tube-like teeth.

If you are hiking in snake country, carry a long stick. If you make a slight noise to warn a snake of your coming it will get out of your way. When climbing be careful not to put your hands on rocky ledges where you cannot see. Mr. Rattler may have chosen that spot to sun himself. (For treatment of a snakebite, see p. 123).

Ticks, bees, wasps, chiggers, scorpions (in the Southwest), and mosquitoes also bother campers at times. Two dangerous spiders are the black widow and the brown recluse. The black widow spider, which has a pea-sized, shiny black body with a red or orange hour-glass shaped marking on the underbelly, likes to live in its irregular web in dark corners. The brown recluse, which has a violin-shaped marking on its back near the head, may live either indoors or outdoors. Indoors, it spins an irregular web in quiet, undisturbed places; outdoors, it usually lives under rocks.

Though these camp pests are annoying and sometimes dangerous, perhaps the worst pest in camp is the careless camper-litterbug.

First Aid

As a cabin counselor, you may be faced with an emergency when far from your campsite. Linda may get her foot sliced while hiking on an overnight. Or Paul may fall while on an outpost trip and break his arm.

If at all possible, take a first aid course from your local American Red Cross chapter before camp begins. Your knowledge of what to do in an emergency may prevent further harm to you or your campers. It may even save a life. It will certainly make you more safety-conscious. Purchase a copy of the

American Red Cross First Aid and Personal Safety or the *First Aid and Emergency Care* textbook; the *Cardiopulmonary Resuscitation* text will also be good to have.

Pack these books with your camp gear. Your camp nurse or doctor may also conduct sessions with your staff in accident-prevention and in what to do in various emergencies.

Be prepared to give emergency care to a camper until you can get him to a doctor, nurse, or hospital. The following emergencies are the most common in camp:

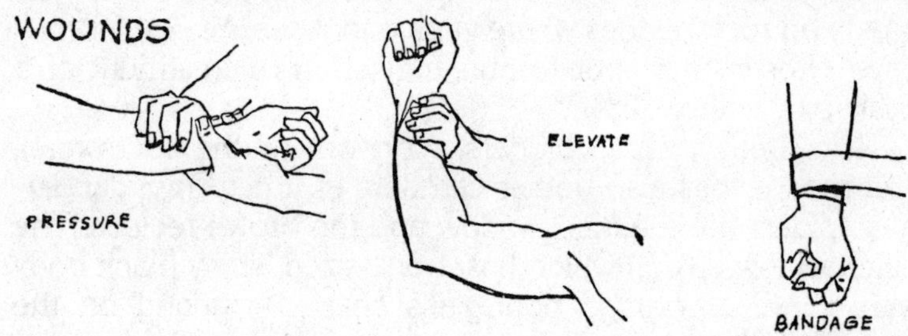

Wounds. If the bleeding is not severe, wash the wound with mild soap and warm water, or boiled water cooled to normal temperature. Apply a sterile dressing and bandage, or a Band-Aid. If the bleeding is severe, apply pressure to the wound with a sterile cloth. When the bleeding stops, put on a dressing and bandage. If an artery or several large veins in the arm are cut, apply pressure on the inner side of the arm midway between the elbow and armpit, pressing the artery against the bone. This diminishes blood pressure below this point. Pressure

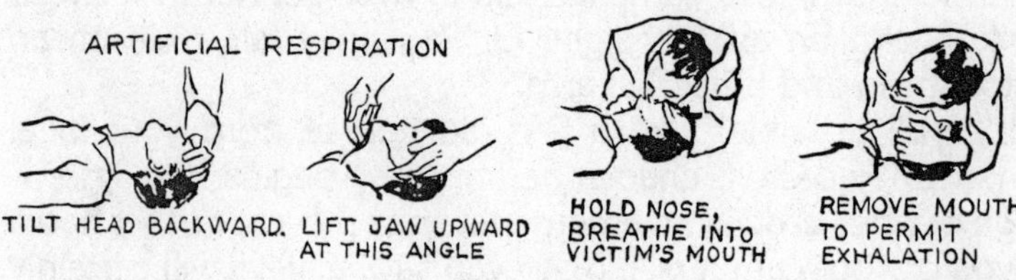

applied to the artery where it crosses the pelvic bone in the groin diminishes bleeding in a leg.

Asphyxiation. The most common causes of breathing stoppage in camp are drowning, electrocution, and overdose of pills; falling into cisterns or abandoned wells where there is insufficient oxygen can also cause asphyxia. Mouth-to-mouth resuscitation is the most effective method of getting air quickly into the lungs. Clear the air passageway, tilt the head back, with chin pointing up, making sure the tongue isn't obstructing the air passageway. Close the victim's nostrils by pinching them with the fingers, and breathe into his mouth. You may close the mouth and breathe into the victim's nostrils if this is easier. But keep the head tilted back to maintain an open airway.

Cardiopulmonary (heart-lung) resuscitation should be learned properly from a qualified instructor and practiced on a mannequin. Breathing can be restored with mouth-to-mouth breathing and circulation can be restored with external cardiac compression. Resuscitation skills can help you save lives not only in camp, but for years to come.

Burns. Encourage campers to avoid sunburn by exposing themselves to the sun's rays gradually and by using a good tanning lotion or oil. A burn from hot coals or boiling water may be more serious. In first- or second-degree burns, submerge the burned area in cold water; do not apply butter, lard, vinegar, etc. But a burn ointment from a first aid kit may be used on first-degree burns. Second-degree burns can be immersed in cold water for one or two hours. Do not use an ointment or spray on a second-degree burn (where there is swelling or blisters). Cover the area with many layers of dry sterile cloth, to keep out the air. If you do not have sterile cloth, you can use pieces of a shirt or scarf and expose them to the direct rays of the sun for ten minutes (or scorch it over a flame, or boil it in water and then dry it). Secure medical help if the burn is severe.

Poison ivy, oak, and sumac. There seems to be no absolute cure for the irritation caused by these plants. After contact, wash the contaminated area with soap and water; a complete change of clothing is also advisable. A calamine solution has a cooling effect. Consult a doctor if the rash keeps spreading, or if the camper's skin is greatly swollen.

Fractures. If a fracture is suspected, immobilize the area of the break and the adjacent joints. No harm is done if there is not a break, but there could be further injury if the person's broken bone is moved. A pole, stick, board, rolled newspaper, magazine, or pillow may be improvised for a splint. The injured person may need to be transported. Shock may be present.

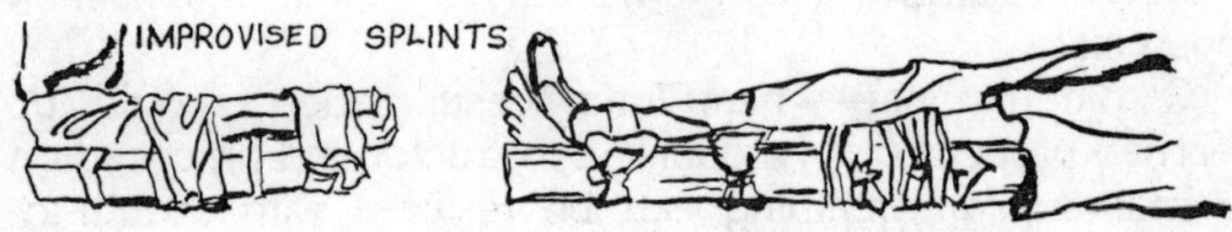

Sprains. If your campground is hilly or rocky, be prepared for sprained ankles. A sprain, an injury to ligaments when they are stretched beyond their normal range of motion, causes heat, swelling, tenderness, and pain when the joint is moved. There may also be a fracture. Elevate the injured part, and apply ice or cold, wet cloths. If movement is necessary, support the joint. The camp nurse will probably have the person x-rayed to be sure there is no further injury.

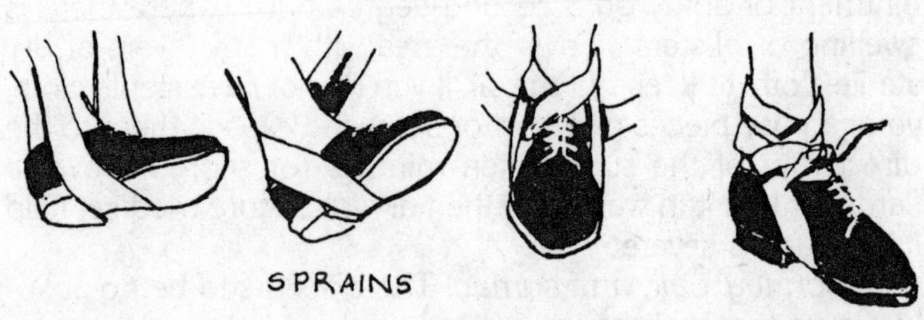

Snakebite. The bite of a nonpoisonous snake gives little pain and causes no more swelling than an ordinary wound. The bite of a coral snake causes slight burning at first, but the bites of other poisonous snakes cause immediate pain and swelling. Instead of teeth marks, poisonous snakes leave one or two puncture wounds. As the poison is absorbed there is general weakness, shortness of breath, nausea, and a weak and rapid pulse. Keep the bitten person quiet. Tie a constricting band above the bite tight enough to stop the spread of venom, but not tight enough to stop circulation. Get medical help as soon as possible.

On an outpost trip you may need to transport an injured person for some distance until help can be secured. Move him as smoothly as possible. Prevent the injured parts from twisting, bending, or shaking. The injured camper may be

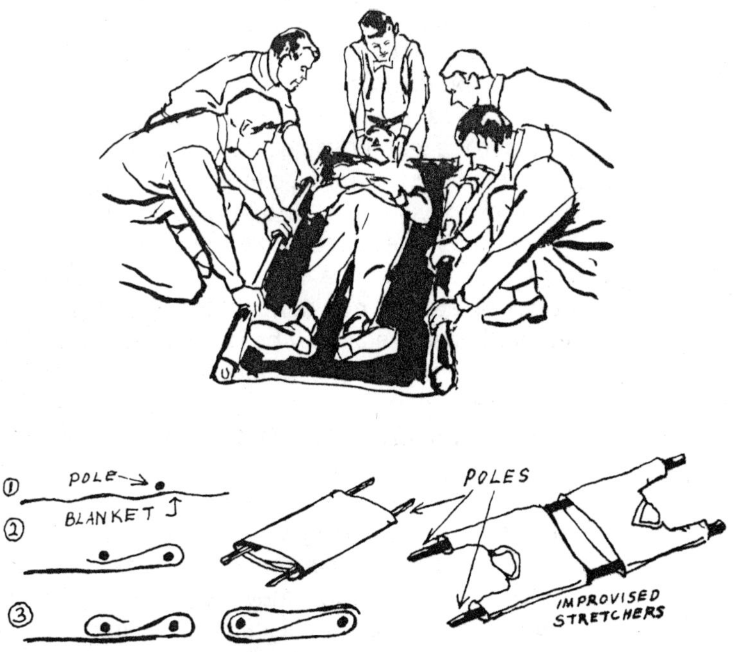

carried by others' hands, or on a blanket. Or a stretcher may be improvised from blankets or two sweat shirts.

If you cannot take a Red Cross course in first aid, obtain a book which describes first aid procedures. Practice some of the skills, and take your book to camp as a reference.

Arts and Crafts

The craft shop can be quite a popular place in camp. Before camp, if possible, become familiar with the various mediums, equipment, and supplies in your craft shop. You may be able to practice making some new project before the campers come to camp.

The craft emphasis at camp should be on creative projects, especially those that use materials native to your site. There may be natural clays for modeling and firing, grasses for weaving, berries for stringing or crushing for dyes, cattails and milkweed for decorations, and bits of bark and cones for shadow boxes. Different craft mediums and techniques should be introduced. Here are some examples:

Leather. It may be braided, woven, stamped, stippled, tooled, carved, stained, painted, dyed, and wood-burned. Some of the numerous leather projects that can be made are belts, purses, Bible covers, lanyards, billfolds, riding crops, key cases, cornb and eyeglass cases, and bookends.

Metal. This includes sheet metal, aluminum and copper, and other wire. Metal may be hammered, form-molded, stamped, embossed, etched, cut, bent, tooled, fluted, spun on a lathe, twisted, and cast. Metal may be used for trays, dishes, bowls, bookends, jewelry boxes, plaques, lamps, planters, knickknacks, coasters, candlesticks, etc. (Of special significance is *copper enameling* which has proved popular in camps. Colored glazes are fused to copper in a kiln. Attractive jewelry items such as earrings, tie clips, pins, bracelets, lockets, and small dishes are fairly easy to make by this method.)

Tin-can craft is a common campcraft since tin cans are plentiful. And the craft program may be tied in with the tripping program by making useful camping equipment. A nest of cooking utensils may be made from different sized cans. Homemade equipment has these advantages: it costs

nothing to make; it may be discarded after use and need not be cleaned. Frying pans, candle holders, water buckets, lanterns, and popcorn poppers may be made. Your campers may also make their own tin cups. Tin cans also make good frames for basket weaving. Tin snips, a hammer, pliers, and canvas gloves are needed for this work.

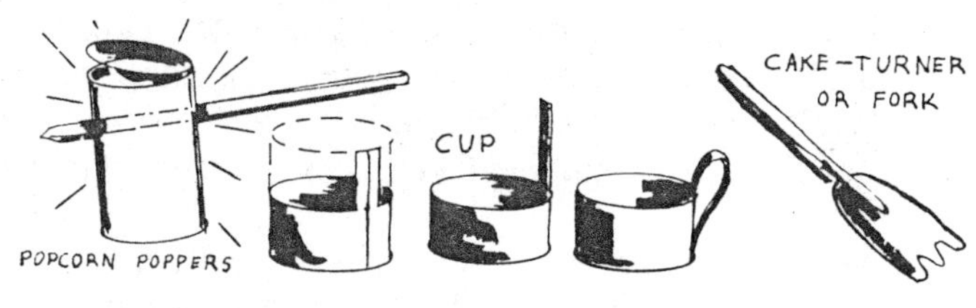

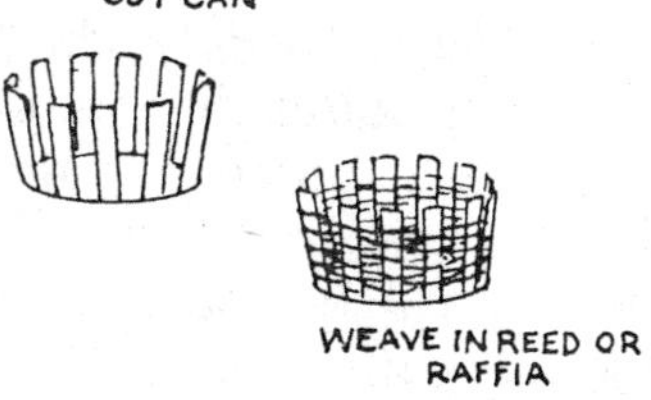

Weaving, braiding, and knotting. Yarns, string, leather thongs, plastic lacing, reed, raffia, twisted crepe paper, grasses, and pine needles can all be used. There can be macrame, loom weaving, coiling, splicing, knitting, and braiding. Belts may be made from string, using square knots. Mats may be made from plaited raffia or grasses. Trays, baskets of all kinds, letter racks, hot pads, seats, and backpacks may be woven.

Fabric printing. Fabrics may be decorated by stenciling, free sketching, tie-dyeing, block-printing, silk screening, batik, and dyeing. Napkins, scarves, place mats, curtains, book covers, and bookmarks may be decorated in these ways.

Plastics may be carved, cut, engraved, cast, drilled, molded, and decorated. Objects can be embedded in liquid plastics, which are then molded into the shapes of ornaments, pins, key chains, etc.

Printing may be done on many mediums with linoleum blocks, wooden blocks, potatoes, and carrots. Leaf prints may be made with permanent inks or dyes. Silk-screen printing is excellent for making insignia items for all in your cabin. Blueprint paper can be used to copy fern and leaf prints.

Bead work. Beads come in various sizes, shapes, and materials. Indian seed beads make Indian jewelry, from rings to belts. Larger beads make place mats, purses, and hot plates.

Wood can be carved, sanded, burned, painted, stained, chip-carved, whittled, and decorated in numerous ways. Picture frames, racks, birdhouses, boxes, bookends, dishes, lamps, bowls, and many other things can be made from wood which is native to your camp. Disks of wood with the bark left on make excellent wall plaques. Birch-bark appliques on a background may be used for outdoor scenes. Rustic benches, stools, candle holders, spoons, forks, and gadgets for outdoor living can be made from spare wood on your grounds.

Sketching is enjoyed by many campers. It can be done with pencil, pen, charcoal, chalk, crayon, and watercolors. Some campers enjoy oils, others sand-painting.

Clays. You are fortunate if there is clay on your campsite. Clay may be used for modeling and for firing. *Ceramics* are popular in camps; objects may be fired in a homemade kiln. Methods used in ceramics include: coil or slab construction, press and pour molding, sculpturing, incising, slip painting, embossing, free form. Pieces may be decorated by sgraffito, incising, and glazing.

Paper can be used to make three-dimensional posters. It may be twisted and woven, braided as yarn, or coiled around jars or bottles. It may be sculptured, twisted, folded, stretched, scalloped, and shellacked. Animals, dolls, plates, bowls, boxes, rattles, masks, and many other things can be made from *papier-mâché.* Crepe paper may be dampened and tooled to look like leather. Decoupage pictures are popular, and kitemaking can be fun.

Felt is used for things such as caps, hairbands, bookmarks, jackets, slippers, purses, belts, mittens, pins, and pencil holders. It is also good for decorating other materials.

Soap carving. Soap is a soft medium for beginning carvers. The finished products can be varnished to give some degree of permanence.

Camp rhythm band instruments may be made in the craft shop. Rattles can be made from gourds, lemme sticks from tree branches, whistles from willow branches, and drums from tin cans.

Stringing beads, seeds, corn, or Indian bead jewelry is a good craft project. Macrame, candle-making, shell crafts, shrink art, ecology boxes, and colored glass hangings make interesting craft shop items. Making *pictures* with *colored sand,* previously dyed, can also be creative fun. Don't forget plaster of paris for plaques and nature prints, cork, tiles, plastic lacing, pipe cleaners, marbles, (cooked) spantex, shells, shadow boxes, feathers, jersey loops, and popsicle sticks are all useful in a craft shop. A *terrarium* to take home gives Mary a bit of the outdoors to keep in her third-floor apartment.

A craft program need not be expensive, but projects should

be useful. Rather than have one project which everyone does at the same time, give campers a choice of several projects. The crafts should be geared to various campers' abilities. Avoid kit projects, ready-to-assemble, and laced projects that stifle ingenuity. Make samples to stimulate your campers' ideas, but encourage them not to copy yours.

Tie the craft program in with other activities in camp, such as the music program, the nature program, and the tripping program. Plan exhibits and give campers an opportunity to make something for someone else. Projects should be finished before they are taken out of the craft shop.

Plan a graded program so that all can have a sense of achievement. Janie may be all thumbs in the craft shop, but she may be a good ball player. A tray, wood-burned and varnished by Janie, may be finished at the same time as Alice's tray which was chip-carved, stained, and varnished. Both girls can have a sense of satisfaction and both can take home well-done and useful projects.

10 Sports and Winter Camping

Games

Campers can learn skills and good attitudes while they're enjoying sports activities in which everyone can take part. There are, however, some things to keep in mind.

Give instructions as simply as possible. Keep in mind the ages, interests, and abilities of your campers. Choose active games whenever possible and plan a wide variety of them. Avoid having too many kinds of formations, such as circles, lineups, count-offs, etc. Use games to help your campers develop the fundamental skills of running, hopping, catching, and throwing.

Tell the name of your game, give clear instructions on how it is played, and allow your campers to ask questions. You may need to demonstrate some games before you play. If confusion occurs, stop and make corrections. If you stop a game while interest is still high, your campers will be eager to play that game again. Strive for easy transitions from one game to another, losing little time dividing into teams, pairing off, etc.

Consider constructing a large outdoor checkerboard with your cabin group, using big wooden disks for checkers. Games like this should be available for campers' free time. Bring to camp ideas for indoor cabin games, puzzles, and games like pick-up-sticks and ring toss. Jack, who may never make the swimming team, may become the champion in a yo-yo tournament. Give each camper an opportunity to excel in some area of camp living.

Many of the highly organized sports (softball, basketball, and touch football) are played frequently back home. More and more camp directors, sensing their campers' craving for adventure and their need to learn new skills, are veering their camp sports programs toward nonplayground activities. If softball games are played, they should not be overemphasized to the neglect of camping skills, trail and outdoor living, and nature interests, which are distinctive camp activities.

Horseback Riding

If horses are a part of your camp's program, a competent instructor should offer classes in horsemanship. Campers who have learned how to ride properly may go on pack trips and overnights, as well as take part in rodeo games.

Hiking

Take along a pair of good hiking shoes and a backpack, if you have one, for camp days are hiking days. A hike may be a short trip to explore your campsite's boundaries, or it may be a trek of several hours to a waterfall, or an all-day trip, with meals cooked out. More experienced hikers may travel for several days through the woods, or to a distant mountaintop.

Basic equipment needed for longer trips includes: lightweight tents, tarps or large sheets of plastic, backpacks, cooking utensils, matches, and dehydrated food packets. Campers usually provide their own ponchos, sleeping bags, mess kits, and canteens. Cooking utensils can be made from tin cans (see p. 163).

The hiking program should be graded, beginning with short hikes. Gradually, as campers gain endurance, the hikes can be lengthened from short walks to all-day trips and then to overnights with meals cooked out.

When hiking along a road, walk single file on the shoulder,

facing traffic. To keep the hikers together, one counselor will be at the front of the line and another at the rear. Slow hikers are usually put in front. Keep the hikers in sight of each other. If a group is large, they may well hike in several smaller groups (each having two or more counselors), so faster hikers can be together and go on ahead. When campers need a break, rest along the way, lying on the ground with feet up.

Wear light clothing when hiking. Take along a jacket or sweat shirt which may be tied around the waist by the sleeves, thus keeping your hands free. Campers can put on jackets when they stop hiking to cool off gradually.

Always take a first-aid kit; this is usually carried at the end of the line by the trailing counselor.

Special kinds of hikes:

Follow-the-leader hike: Hikers go over, under, and around obstacles, following their hike leader.

Beeline hike: Sight a distant fire tower or tree and hike in a straight line over all terrain toward that point. Hikers may not go around objects.

Orienteering hike: Using a Silva compass and topographical map, set out for a destination on the map.

Photography hike: Hike along country roads or cross-country. The object is to get good photographs that, when put together, will tell a story.

Nature hike: A list of nature specimens is given to each group of hikers. Each group starts at a different time, and their object is to collect all of these specimens along the way.

Exploration hike: Campers love to explore a stream, an abandoned railroad bed, or follow mountain trails or a footpath. Explorations may be combined with nature hikes.

Compass hike: Campers must know how to read a compass and a topographical map. They should check their paces beforehand, to know the length of their strides. A trail is laid previously by a group of campers or a counselor. A compass reading such as 140° may start a camper on his way. If his compass reading is accurate and he paced off 40 feet correctly, he will arrive at the location of his next marker, which will give him another compass reading and distance.

Trips may be made on foot, by bicycle, by horseback, by canoe, and even by covered wagons.

Archery

If a skilled leader heads the archery program at camp, this activity can be most attractive to campers. Instruction should be given in how to string a bow, how to stand, and how to nock the arrow. Teach campers to observe all safety regulations and to handle bows and arrows as weapons. Never allow a camper to shoot without proper supervision. (The Camp Archery Association, 200 Coligni Avenue, New Rochelle, N.Y. 10800 can provide helpful information in setting up a camp program.)

Set up a field archery course as well as a target range. Swing sandbags from trees, vary the distances to targets, place targets in trees and in ravines. Archers should shoot from different positions. For an unusual test of skill, you might even want to combine a hike with your archery in a field course.

Riflery

Does your camp have a rifle range? If so, there should be time during pre-in-camp training for staff members who are not familiar with rifles to learn something about safe rifle-handling. The more you can learn about such camp activities before camp, the better you will be able to interest your campers in them. If you don't know how to care for and clean a rifle properly, as well as how to shoot it, you'll have fun learning.

Here are some basic riflery rules:

1. Never point a gun, loaded or otherwise, at anything you do not intend to shoot.
2. No rifle should be loaded until the shooter is in firing position on the line, with his rifle pointed at the target, and the command is given to load.
3. At the command "Cease fire," a camper unloads his rifle, opens the action, and lays his rifle down, with the muzzle pointing toward the target.
4. No one may walk in front of the firing line.
5. Before any commands are given, campers waiting their turn to shoot must be seated behind the firing line.

The National Rifle Association has a 10-point safety code which must be practiced by campers in their riflery program. This association, which has an excellent graded program for camps, offers pins and brassards to campers who qualify for these awards. The NRA also offers help in setting up your camp program and in qualifying your instructors. (You may write to the National Rifle Association, 1600 Rhode Island Avenue, N.W., Washington, D.C. 20036.)

Waterfront

Perhaps the most popular place in camp is the waterfront. Many campers come to camp to swim, others to learn to swim. Camp should provide plenty of opportunities to learn waterfront skills.

Swimming

Waterfront regulations at your camp might look something like this:

1. There is swimming only when lifeguards are on duty.
2. Campers swim within designated areas.
3. At buddy check, all swimming and talking stops. Each camper finds his buddy immediately; they hold up each other's hand.
4. There is no swimming under the diving boards.
5. Campers sit down on the slide and go down one at a time.
6. One whistle blast means a buddy call; three means that all get out of the water immediately.
7. No throwing of sand on the beach is permitted.
8. No ducking of campers or unnecessary roughness is allowed.
9. Your buddy tags must be moved to the "in" side of the checkboard before entering the water. Your tags must be returned to the "out" side when you leave the water.

Learn these rules before camp begins; post them in your cabin during camp.

Some type of safety system for checking on swimmers should be used in all camps. There may be roll calls before and after swim for a small camp. Checkboards may be used with larger groups. Campers may go through a turnstile, so

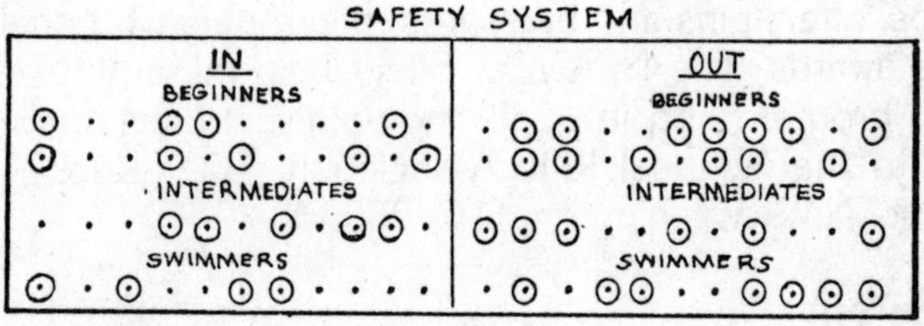

SAFETY SYSTEM

IN	OUT
BEGINNERS	BEGINNERS
INTERMEDIATES	INTERMEDIATES
SWIMMERS	SWIMMERS

that all must go by the checkboard. As a double check, some waterfront directors insist that each camper watches his buddy move his tag on the board.

The buddy system requires all campers to be paired with a buddy of the same swimming ability, so that they both swim in the same area. When the whistle is blown for a buddy check, campers may be counted in each swimming area and the totals verified with the checkboard.

In girls' camps sometimes a colored cap system is used. These may be cheap tank caps, loaned to campers or sold at a low price. Blue or green caps may be given to advanced swimmers, red to intermediates, and white to nonswimmers. Guards can be spotted quickly if they wear yellow caps.

Preliminary swim tests should be given to all campers on arrival, so they may be placed in the proper swim classes and limited to certain areas of water according to their swimming ability.

The waterfront should be run by a waterfront director who holds a current American Red Cross Water Safety Instructor's card or a YMCA Instructor's rating. There should be 1 qualified lifeguard on duty for every 10 campers in the water. If your camp is short on guards, the difficulty can be overcome by having campers swim in smaller groups which can be adequately guarded.

Waterfront practices should comply with the American Red Cross or YMCA standards. If the swimming area is a pool, the water should be tested regularly.

If a lake or stream is used, the water should be clear enough for one to see to a depth of at least five feet. The bottom should slope gradually and be free from muck, stumps, holes, debris, and underwater growth. The water should also be tested for purity.

Safety lines should be used to define nonswimmer, beginner, and swimming and diving areas. Docks and guard stations should be located for maximum safety of campers.

Refreshments should not be brought to the beach area.

Good first-aid equipment should be kept at the beach house and someone on the beach staff should have first aid training. Ring buoys, poles, whistles, lifeboats, megaphones, and possibly surfboards should be available at strategic locations for the lifeguards' use.

If you are a nonswimmer yourself, try to learn to swim. At least overcome any fear of the water and try to pass your beginner's test during pre-in-camp training. Take this opportunity to pick up a few pointers from the waterfront staff before camp. (In some camps, swim classes and classes in lifesaving are open to staff as well as campers.)

Boating

Become familiar with your camp's watercraft and know the regulations concerning the use of each type of boat. In general the following regulations apply:

1. Boats should not enter the swimming area.
2. Passing a swimming test in deep water is a prerequisite for using boats. Nonswimmers wearing life jackets may go out in rowboats.
3. Boats should never carry more than their safe loads.
4. No standing up in boats is permitted.
5. All boats are to be beached at the sign of an oncoming thunderstorm.
6. All boats should be kept in good condition.
7. All power boats must comply with state regulations and carry prescribed safety equipment.

To be able to take rowboats away from camp on a trip, campers should demonstrate their ability to enter, launch, and row in both a straight line and a maze course. They should be instructed to hold onto the side of a rowboat if it should capsize.

Canoes

An American Red Cross canoeing course or some other instruction should be given in handling a canoe. Canoeists should have their Intermediate swimming certificates or be able to support themselves in deep water for 10 minutes while wearing shirt and jeans (or trousers). Campers should learn how to board, launch, and dock a canoe from a dock or from a beach. They should practice handling and carrying the canoe on shore, in preparation for portages.

Campers should know the bow, backwater, sweep and reverse sweep, draw and pushover, and J strokes; and should be able to demonstrate the bow rudder, cross bow rudder, sculling, and draw. They should demonstrate their ability to handle canoes both tandem and solo. They should practice swamping, hand-paddling, and swimming the canoe to shore. They must know how to change places in a canoe, vault overboard, rescue a tired swimmer, and do a canoe-over-canoe rescue of a swamped canoe. In preparation for a canoe trip, campers should be able to demonstrate wind-paddling, correcting trim, formation paddling, reentering a canoe from deep water, and have taken a five-mile paddle.

Kayaks are handled somewhat similarly to canoes and should be used only by swimmers.

Sailboats

Sailing should be reserved for good swimmers who have received instruction from a qualified small-craft instructor. Some safety precautions when using sailboats: Always keep the mainsheet so it can be unfastened quickly. Jibe only in a light wind and shorten the sail when necessary. Do not sail in a thunderstorm.

All watercraft should stay within sight of camp or within designated limits unless used for tripping, in which case waterfront personnel will be aboard. The number of sailboats and their sizes and types will be determined by the number of campers, the kind of waterfront and beach area you have, your budget, and the program you offer. Favorite camp sailboats include: Funfish, Sunfish, Sailfish, Lightning, Snipe, Star, Penguin, Frostbite, Sprite, catboats, and catamarans.

Water-skiing

In this sport proper instruction should be given, using proper equipment. Swimming tests are a prerequisite to water-skiing. An observer, in addition to the driver, should be in the power boat when it is pulling a skier, who should wear a life jacket or belt.

Windsurfing

This sport, in which a sail on a surfboard can send you skimming across the lake, is gaining interest in camps. Campers can learn to balance and maneuver their craft in a short time. But only good swimmers should participate and life jackets should be worn.

Scuba-diving

Offered in some camps, scuba-diving should be reserved for good swimmers and offered only under competent instruction. The use of face masks, snorkels, and compressed air tanks should be limited to campers who have passed tests that demonstrate their ability to use such equipment. (A swimmer should be able to put a mask on under water and clear it.) Toy equipment should not be used. (Such floating devices as air mattresses, inner tubes, and inflatable toys should not be allowed in the water.)

Special waterfront programs

Since the waterfront is a favorite spot for campers, it can well become the center of many special activities. Games of *water polo, water basketball,* and less organized games such as *Red Rover* and *water ball* are all popular. *Water carnivals* and *pageants* may grow out of the instructional program. A carnival can offer waterfront games for landlubbers, beginners, intermediates, swimmers, and divers. Relays with spoons and peanuts, open umbrellas and Ping-Pong balls, can be a part of the program, plus comic diving exhibitions.

Boats and canoes can be used in contests of *tilting, swamping, jumping in and out,* and *racing.* War canoes, whaleboats, and sailboats are fun to race. *Maze courses* around buoys, and *slalom races* may challenge some campers.

In some camps the advanced swimming class develops its own pageant with music, synchronized swimming, and a story to go with it. Sometimes the story has to do with their own experiences at camp. Or they may present a children's story such as "The Three Bears," "Sleeping Beauty," "Cinderella," or "Hiawatha." Here's a way to challenge the creativity of your campers and provide a medium for expression and participation, as well as skill development.

Canoe-tripping

Canoe-tripping is a climactic event for campers who are experienced in campcraft and canoeing skills. To be eligible for such a trip, campers should complete a Red Cross or similar course in canoeing and demonstrate successfully their skills in campcraft, first aid, and lifesaving. Cookouts, overnights, and short trips out of camp are preparation for a canoe trip of three days to a week or more.

After campers and staff have qualified for the trip, the group plans the route with the help of topographical or trip maps, the distance, and the number of days required to make the trip. Campers work on menus, programming, and organizing, and plan how they will pack and carry gear.

After the route is planned, camper leaders (a trip master and two staff members) should go on a scouting trip to locate overnight sites, and to check for water levels, currents, channels, leeward sides of islands, possible portages, rapids, places of interest along the way, wood supply, drinking water, swimming areas, and possible meal spots.

The scouts check the timing of the trip and mark their maps accordingly. They establish communication spots, locate phones and get phone numbers, and establish emergency meeting places where camp cars can pick up a sick or injured camper. They also secure permission for campfires and for crossing private property.

When packing for the trip, keep the gear lightweight and use waterproof plastic bags for almost everything. Use backpacks or wooden boxes that fit into canoes and can be carried on paddles if portaging is necessary. Pack your personal gear into your sleeping bag. Waterproof the matches and pack them in several places in case one pack gets wet. Pack your food by meals, so you won't have to unload all your gear at each meal. Keep snack food, such as raisins, nuts, and dried fruit, in easy-to-reach places. Keep your first aid kit accessible.

You may include in your *shared equipment* the following: canoes in good condition (16- to 18-foot canoes are best for tripping; these hold two or three campers with their gear and equipment), an extra paddle for each one or two canoes, tents or tarps, ax, saw, rope, bug repellent, Halizone tablets, carborundum stone, first-aid kit, shovel, toilet paper, pots, pans, soap, candle, dish towel, matches, food.

For *personal gear* you may include: sleeping bag (air mattress or foam pad optional), poncho, brimmed hat, jacket or sweat shirt, socks, jeans, shorts, swimsuit, underwear, pajamas, tennis shoes or moccasins, toilet articles (soap, comb, etc.), cup, plate, jackknife, fork, spoon, Bible or Testament, floating flashlight, sunglasses, suntan lotion.

How much clothing you take will be determined by how long you will be gone. But keep it to a minimum; you can wash along the way.

Someone should bring a harmonica or uke. You may want your camera, a notebook and pencil, fishing gear, and possibly binoculars.

When packing the canoe, keep the equipment low. Cover it

with a tarp or poncho. Watch the trim of your canoe. In a strong wind you may need to reposition yourself and your gear. Logs or an inflated air mattress in the bottom of your canoe will keep your gear out of standing water in case it rains.

Organize your trip. Choose from among the campers a trip master who will be responsible for the group. There should be at least two or three counselors along, more if the group is large. A nurse or other first-aider should also be part of the group. Set up committees (shelter and gear, food, fire, and cleanup) so that everyone has a job to do. A program committee will plan evening programs for your overnight stops.

Start out with your stronger paddlers in the stern position. Eventually all should take turns. One counselor should be in the lead canoe and one in the trailing canoe. Canoes should stay in single file, 25-30 feet apart. Other formations may be taken when it is safe to do so. Establish some signals for communication. (A raised paddle may mean, "Look over there!")

Along the trip, be sensitive to your group's needs. They may tire early on their first day out. On a hot day, you may want to stop and swim along the way. Above all, relax and enjoy yourselves and the outdoors God created for you. You may choose to make a picture story of your trip. Keep a log of events along the way.

Evening programs may include stunts, contests, games, stories, singing, discussions, sharing from the Word, praise, and prayer.

On returning, evaluate your trip while it is still fresh in everyone's mind. Your evaluation should include the food, the social values, the route, the pace and timing, skills learned along the way, program, equipment, leadership, and spiritual growth.

Clean and return all equipment right away. After the last paddle has been stored on the rack, and the last pot washed and dried, it is hot showers and sleep for happy, tired campers who have a trip full of wonderful memories to store away for the rest of their lives.

Winter Camping

Many camps are winterizing their buildings so their facilities can be used year-round rather than only two or three months during the summer. Using facilities year-round can be more economical and can enlarge the ministry of the summer camp. School vacations and weekends provide time for campers to enjoy winter activities as well as summer ones.

In winter the bugs and snakes are gone. Everything is peaceful and quiet in a blanket of white, and camp is most inviting. But winter camping is different in other ways too.

Keep warm. Your first concern in cold weather is keeping warm. The chilling effect of low temperatures can be increased by the force of the wind. At 30° F. with a wind of 20 mph, the wind chill is 4° F., the temperature exposed skin feels. A 20 mph wind at 0° will have the effect of -39° F. on exposed skin.

Insulate your body by dressing in several layers of "breathable," not plastic or rubber-coated clothing. The dead air space created by the layers of clothing prevents loss of body heat yet allows moisture to escape. Wool is a good insulation since the kinky fibers trap the air. Wool also tends to restrict heat conduction when wet and is more comfortable than cotton which often gets sodden and sticks to you. When you are active, a layer or two may be removed. When you stop to rest, another layer may be put on.

The lightest weight material for the amount of warmth is duck or goose down, but be sure your down jacket or sleeping bag is kept dry. You will need to keep a water-repellent parka handy for heavy snow or rain. Though it is the warmest of sleeping bags, a down bag will require an air mattress or foam pad underneath since the weight of your body compacts the down and destroys the loft which makes it so warm. Of course, when you roll over the down springs back and fluffs up again.

Keep your head covered. Your head needs a greater blood

supply than other parts of your body. It may sound strange, but if your feet are cold, put on a hat.

Two lightweight sweaters tend to be warmer than one heavy sweater. Clothing should fit loosely to provide freedom of movement. Long wool underwear is good; if you are allergic to wool, use fishnet or waffle weave clothing next to your skin.

Jeans are common dress for summer, but they are not best for winter camping, though they will do for short trips when worn over long underwear. Buy them a size or two larger than you normally wear and try not to get them wet in the snow—wet jeans can make you miserable in cold weather.

For your hands, mittens are warmer than gloves. Better still, wear gloves inside your mittens.

Always change your clothing at night if you want to sleep warm. If you go to sleep in the clothes you have been wearing, the day's accumulated moisture will evaporate during the night and keep you cold. A jogging outfit or sweat suit makes good sleeping apparel, especially if the jacket is hooded.

Boots will be one of your most expensive items of clothing. Be sure they fit well, give good ankle support, and are broken in before you wear them on a trip. Buy them for the kind of winter camping you'll be doing. Snowmobile boots have felt liners, rubber soles, and nylon tops that are tied around the leg to keep out loose snow. Oiled leather insulated boots with vibrim lug soles are good for hiking in rough terrain or over rocks. Several pairs of socks will not only keep you warmer, but also help prevent blisters. A pair of wool socks and a pair of cotton terry-lined ones makes a good combination. The felt liners are good in severe weather.

Keep dry. Water conducts heat—or cold—240 times greater than air. Do not overdress so that you perspire or you will chill too quickly. If you get wet, go inside and dry out or change clothing immediately. If this is not possible, build a fire and stay near it until you are dry.

If you are backpacking in cold weather (and this is great fun) choose your tent wisely. A tent with an open front such as a baker tent will allow you to enjoy the warmth of your campfire. A mountain tent with snow flaps can be anchored in a strong wind by piling snow along the flaps. A frost liner inside the tent will prevent the moisture that forms on the inside from getting on your sleeping bag, but will also add a good bit to the weight in your pack.

Keep rested. Don't allow yourself to get overly tired when outside in cold weather. In order to keep your energy level up you will need to get plenty of rest—and food.

Eat well. When your blood sugar drops in warm weather, you may feel tired and have less stamina. In cold weather, it will also be difficult to maintain body temperature. Backpacking in cold weather requires careful menu planning. Dehydrated, freeze-dried, or lightweight foods will take up less room in a pack, but you will need more fats and carbohydrates to give fuel.

It will be harder to start a fire in the open since you must get the tinder up to kindling temperature, so take along a candle, trench candle, or canned heat. Better yet, a small backpacker's stove will be worth its weight in cold weather. Use large, waterproofed, kitchen matches, or you can buy waterproof and windproof matches. Before you chop wood in very cold weather, warm the ax-head to prevent breakage.

Plan well. Plan ahead for emergencies. Leave a trip plan with someone, and never winter-camp alone. Two or three adults should go with any group of campers. Be sure you know the terrain and are familiar with the use of map and compass. The woods will look different in winter than they did in summer.

Take extra flashlight batteries—cold weather shortens battery life. Tape the switch in the *off* position if your flashlight will be carried in a pack, so it won't accidently be turned on in the daytime.

Emergency procedures. Know how to recognize frostbite and what to do if someone develops it. Frostbite strikes those least protected parts of the body—hands, feet, ears, and face. Frostbite first appears as white spots or grayish yellow areas, and the skin has a glossy surface. Never rub a frostbitten area, for there is always danger of injuring the frozen flesh which may then become gangrenous. Thaw the frozen area slowly in warm water (102-105° F.) or, if the fingers are frostbitten, by having the sufferer warm his hand in his armpits.

If you fall through ice, reach out as far as possible to distribute your weight, creep out onto the ice and roll away from the area. Rolling in a snow bank will act as a blotter. Get warm and dry as soon as possible.

To reach someone who has fallen through ice, creep out on your stomach and extend a pole or ladder to him. Tie a rope around yourself, so you can be pulled back should the ice crack.

Activities. Winter camping offers its own special activities such as skiing (downhill and cross-country), tobogganing, snowmobiling, ice fishing, ice boating, sledding, skating, or inner tubing. For those less adventuresome there is winter hiking, snow sculpture, or a snowball war. You can slide down an icy hill on almost anything or play crack the whip with a chain of sleds pulled by a snowmobile. And some winter games require no equipment at all.

Things to remember. Keep safety uppermost in your planning. Don't schedule too tightly. Allow plenty of time for interaction between campers and staff. Allow time to sit in front of the fireplace and think and dream. Have your campfire programs with no electricity—just firelight. Bible study groups can lounge casually around the fire and discuss. Provide lots of hot chocolate and plenty of good hot food. Keep roaring fires blazing in your fireplaces all the time, and winter camp will lure campers from far and near to your campsite.

11
Stress Camping

Stress camping and survival camping are growing programs in evangelical camps today. Some have called today's youth a pampered generation. We push a button to entertain ourselves on a screen; we push another button to cook our meals in minutes in a microwave oven. We live in a plastic, throwaway society where there is little to challenge campers. Many feel they have tried everything, seen everything, gone everywhere and they come to camp questioning what new experiences camp can offer.

Stress camping can challenge the camper to try something that may be difficult or at first seem impossible. He can learn a deeper meaning of trust when his life depends on that bowline knot he has tied, or when his buddy belays him off a cliff. Stress situations can increase dependence on the Lord as well as develop personal confidence. The camper will increase his physical fitness through better coordination and agility. The development of problem-solving skills is encouraged. Through group cooperation he will learn to appreciate the contribution of others. More emphasis is placed on cooperation and improvement of individual skills than on competition.

Some conditioning exercises should be given prior to

strenuous or vigorous experiences, and for these activities some advance construction may be necessary.

Tests of Individual Skill

The Balance Beam

These can be arranged into a course of inclines and level or descending cat walks. Walks can be of different lengths. Posts should be sunk into the ground for stability.

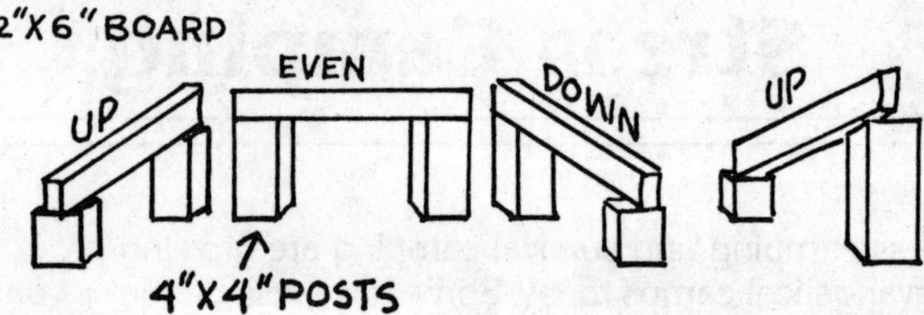

The Crawl

Campers crawl along ropes anchored between two sturdy trees.

The Swing

Campers move from one swinging log to another. For a variation of this use automobile tires. Logs or tires should be at least two feet off the ground.

The Ladder

This is a difficult balancing feat so old mattresses or tumbling mats should be placed underneath. One-inch dowels are placed about 14 inches apart for rungs of the ladder. Rungs should be lashed securely to rope sides. Rings should allow ladder to flip over easily.

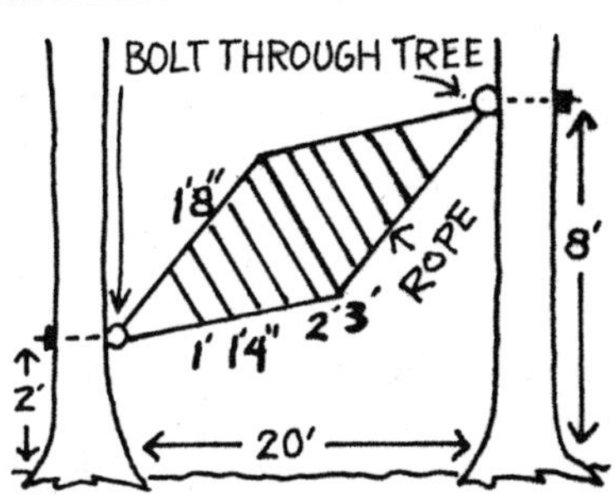

The Swinging Log

Allow free swinging of log but tether it so it cannot hit the trees.

Stump Jump

Stumps should be at least a foot in diameter and far enough apart so that campers cannot quite step from one to another.

Rope Bridge

Campers walk across a rope bridge attached between two sturdy trees.

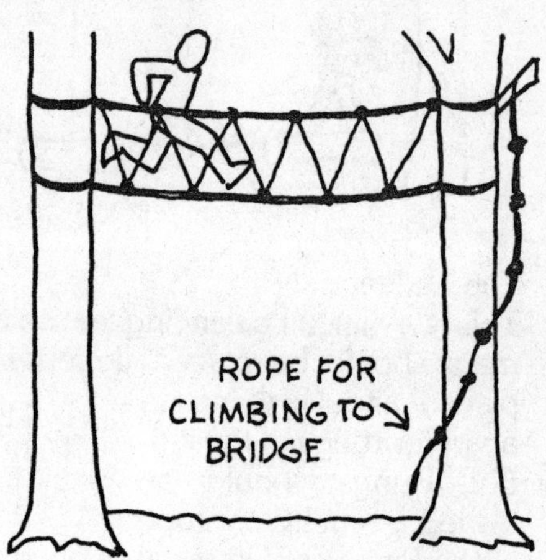

Swing into Net

Campers swing on rope and let go at the height of the swing, landing in a net. The distance from the net to the rope is dependent on the length of the rope and the height of the swing. Test carefully first.

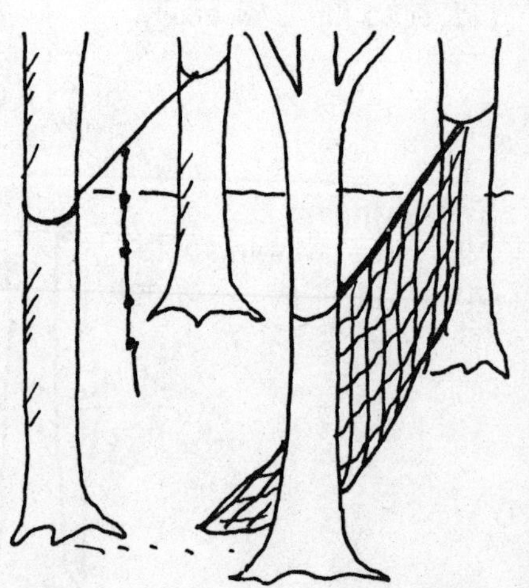

Free Fall

Campers put their wrists through rope slings attached to a caribiner which slides down the free fall rope. Campers jump off platform and free fall from the tree. Spotters are ready to catch shorter campers who cannot reach the ground at the bottom of the fall.

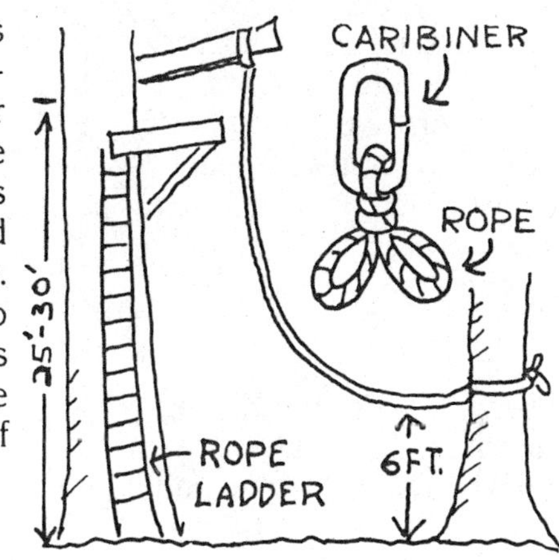

Zip Line

This is similar to the free fall, but a wire is used instead of rope and the trip is faster. Spotters should be used in the water and by the ladder.

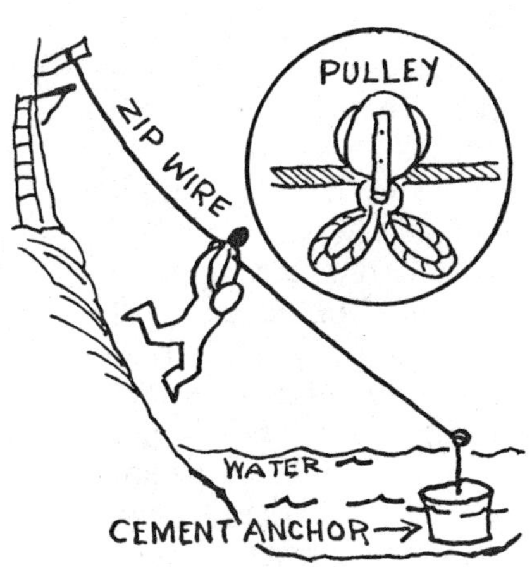

Problem-solving Group Activities

Electric Fence

All participants must get over the fence without touching the wire or going under it. Trees are considered "electrified" also. If a camper touches the wire, he is considered "dead" and must start over. Anyone in contact with him is also "dead." The whole group must get over the "electric" fence.

Rock Climbing

Rappelling is an exhilarating activity for the camper who thinks he has tried everything else. You *must* have a skilled and experienced instructor to offer this activity. A rock cliff, the wall of a building, or a constructed rappel wall may be used. No climb should be attempted alone, and the climber should always be on belay. It requires a conscious effort to get hurt on a properly set up rappel, but the camper needs to learn the proper knots, where to tie the anchor point, where to clip on, which hand goes where, and how to construct the Swiss seat or harness. Proper equipment must also be used —climbing ropes, caribiners, brakes, bars, etc.

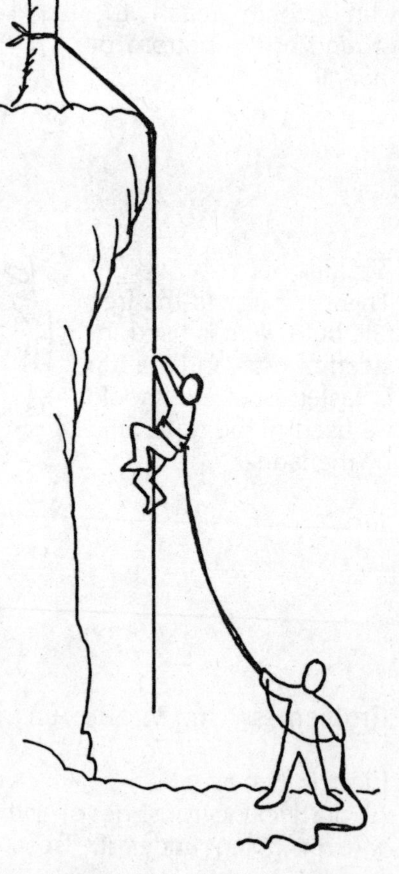

For specific instructions see the *Beginner's Guide to Rock and Mountain Climbing* by Ruth and John Mendenhall (Stackpole, 1975).

Cat Walk
The object is for the group to walk a prescribed distance without touching the ground with any part of the body.

Automobile Tire
The object is for the group to get the automobile tire over the 16-foot pole.

The Wall
The object is to get all the campers over the wall as quickly as possible. No aids are allowed, but campers may assist each other. Trees may not be climbed.

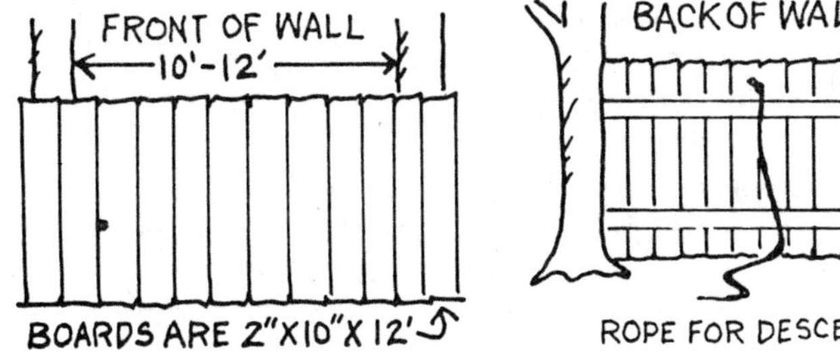

Obstacle Course

This can be an individual test or a timed group test. Campers may run over balance beams, cross a log over a mud puddle or water hole, climb a rope ladder, run through auto tires, and squirm under ropes a foot off the ground. Design your own course, but keep the safety of campers uppermost.

Positive mental carry-over as well as sheer enjoyment result from successfully accomplishing the stress camping program. Of course risk is involved and therefore the camper's safety must be kept in mind in the planning stages, but the high rewards of confidence, self-worth, and well-being must be weighed against the risk.

In survival camping, the camper learns the skills of map and compass; use of the ax, saw, and knife; outdoor cooking; fire building; shelters; knots; lashing; first aid; and knowledge of plants, animals, and fish in the area. (These are discussed in more detail in chapters 12 and 13.) The camper learns what is edible and how to prepare it. He learns what to avoid. Some camps complete their survival training with a one- or two-day solo. Each camper spends a day or longer alone in the woods using the survival skills he has learned. He constructs his own shelter and lives off the land eating whatever he finds that is edible. He has a lot of time to think, to integrate his skills, to talk to the Lord, and to set goals for his life. The solo is usually the highlight of his camping experience, and is generally followed by a sharing time and a banquet.

Challenge your campers to attempt the difficult, the seemingly impossible, and they may learn the meaning of trust, that with the Lord's help the impossible can become possible. Philippians 4:13—"I can do everything through Him [Christ] who gives me strength"—can become a reality in their lives.

12
Camping Skills

Every camper, including you, needs to learn outdoor skills, for they are basic to true camp living. You and the rest of the camp staff should have some knowledge of camping skills before the campers arrive. If you can, practice some of the skills described in this chapter even before precamp training. If you're familiar with the skills, you can help your campers become more resourceful and self-reliant in the outdoors. Don't deny them the satisfying experiences of sleeping out, setting up camp, preparing meals, taking care of gear, and matching their wits against wind, weather, and water.

Whether your trip will be by land or water, discuss the where, when, and how of your journey before starting out. Preparation and prerequisites for a trip by water have already been discussed. Preparation for a trip by land is similar—you need to plan what gear and shelters you'll need, to divide up responsibilities, etc. Plan the trip *with* your campers, and their enthusiasm will run high.

Choosing a Campsite

Look for a high spot that's level and provides good drainage. Avoid gullies which may become flooded. If you pitch your tent facing the morning sun, it will dry out quickly from the night's dampness. Facing the tent east or south will also usually prevent the wind from driving rain into the tent, but know the area's prevailing winds.

Do not pitch your tent directly under a large tree, or a dead tree. Dead branches may fall in a storm. And if a tree is tall, it may be struck by lightning.

Avoid pitching camp near tall underbrush which may house flies and insects. Don't camp under overhanging cliffs, and be sure you can recognize poison ivy before you roll out your sleeping bag. Be on the lookout for anthills and yellow jacket nests; ants are annoying, but angry yellow jackets can inflict painful stings. Nearby potholes or marshes may be inhabited by hungry mosquitoes that are just waiting for you. If you camp 10-20 feet above the water level of a lake you will avoid the morning mist off the lake, yet, you may catch a gentle breeze that will help keep flying pests away.

Fire-building

Fires are used for cooking, heating water, warmth, destroying garbage and trash, for light, and for campfire fellowship. Select a clearing in the woods, making sure you have an unobstructed view of the sky. Dig down through the topsoil to clay or rock to form a pit, or build your fire on sand or rock (not shale, which may explode when heated). Your fire circle should be cleared up to a diameter of 6-10 feet of leaves, grass, and everything that burns.

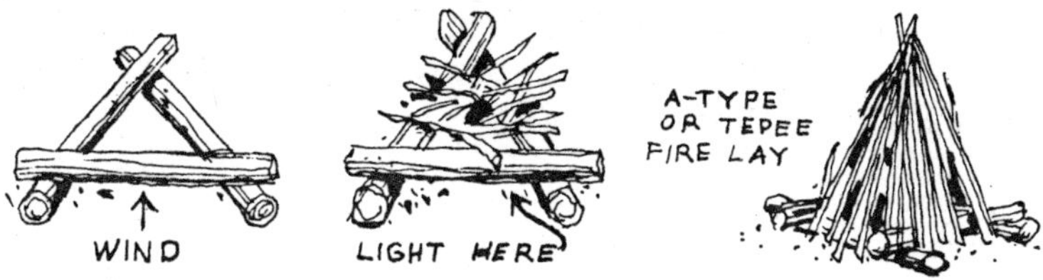

Before lighting your fire, have something on hand to put it out, such as a bucket of water, or sand and a shovel. Before striking that match, gather all the wood you think you will need; then gather more. Set up a woodpile with wood cut to usable lengths, stacked neatly. Divide your woodpile into sections for the different sizes of wood.

Tinder is material that will burn right from the match. It is small twigs, up to matchstick thickness. Goldenrod tops, blueberry twigs, dead pine needles, cones of some evergreens, and birch bark also make good tinder.

Kindling is piled next. This is wood up to the thickness of your thumb, 6-12 inches long.

Fuel is bigger wood and logs.

You can tell what kind of camper a person is by looking at his woodpile. Set up the woodpile as soon as you arrive at a camping spot. A tarp over the woodpile will insure dry wood in case of rain later on.

Good wood for burning will snap when broken. If a stick merely bends, it is still green and will be difficult to burn. If it crumbles, it is rotted and has little fuel value.

Softwoods burn rapidly and give quick, hot fires; but such fires require much fuel. Some fast-growing softwood trees are pine, spruce, hemlock, tamarack, fir, larch, and cedar.

The hardwoods are slower burning and give good coals for roasting. These are the slower-growing deciduous trees with harder, more compact wood. Some hardwood trees are oak, maple, ash, elm, locust, beech, and hickory.

Begin your fire with a basic fire lay, an A-type or a tepee. From this basic lay, you can build your fire gradually into the type of fire that will best serve your purpose.

When lighting a fire, stand with the wind to your back. Hold your flaming match under the tinder. Remember that fire burns up, so your kindling should be above the tinder. Build your fire gradually, piece by piece. Do not build a fire any bigger than you will need. A rookie camper will build a big fire and then can't get close enough to toast his marshmallow.

Types of fires

The *tepee* is good for a quick, hot fire where concentrated heat is needed. It's a fine fire for cooking a one-pot meal or for boiling water.

For a *log cabin fire,* lay logs to form a square. Larger logs go on the bottom. Build toward the center as you lay each square. This fire gives good light for a campfire and may be set up before lighting. A small tepee in the center will ignite the logs.

A *crisscross* fire is similar to the log cabin, but except for the first four logs, the wood is laid on solid. This is a long-burning fire that yields a good bed of coals when it burns down. Graduate the size of the sticks as you do for the log cabin fire.

A *star* fire is an Indian fire. It is used when one wants a fire to burn for a long time. Once the fire is started, little fuel is needed. You merely kick the logs toward the center as they burn.

For a *hunter's* fire, place two green logs almost, but not quite, parallel to each other. This will give a good draft for the fire that is built between the green logs. Several pots can be placed on the fire at one time, or a crane may be built over the fire for hanging pots. Either way, it's a convenient fire for larger groups of people.

A *trench* fire is good on a hot or windy day because the fire is in the ground. When the weather is very warm, you can stand out of the direct heat while you are cooking. When it's windy, the trench protects the flame. Several pots can be heated at one time over this fire, so it is also useful for larger groups.

A *reflector* fire is half a tepee fire. It is good for baking or for using a reflector oven. A flat rock or green logs make a good reflector. For greater heat reflection, use a sheet of metal or aluminum foil.

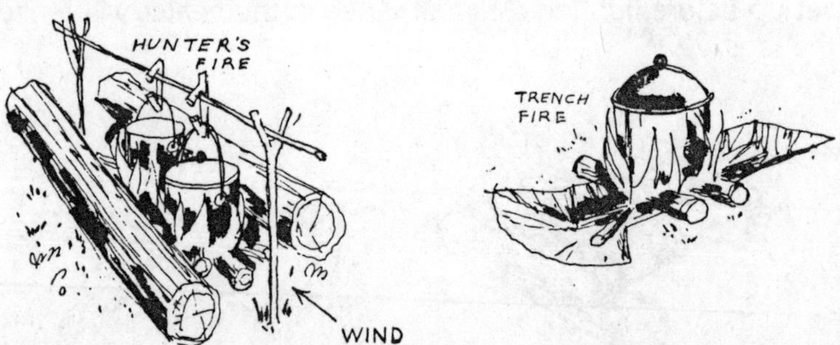

An *emu* or *bean-hole* fire is used for cooking in a hole in the ground. Actually a crisscross or log cabin fire is ignited near the hole. When there are red coals, the fire is brushed into the hole. Dig the hole three times as large as your pot. You may line the hole with flat rocks to help hold the heat. Be sure your pot is surrounded top, bottom, and sides with live coals.

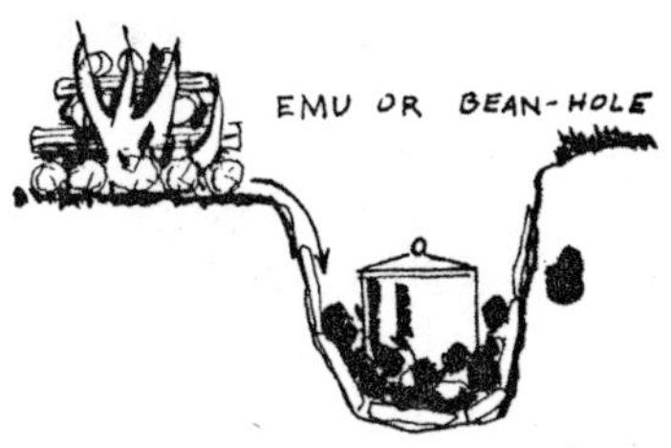

Fires in wet weather. Did you ever try to build a fire with wet wood, or while it's raining? There are ways of starting that fire with little trouble, even when the wood is wet.

1. Birch bark will light from a match even if you have to shake the water off.
2. Split a wet log; the center will be dry.
3. Make a fuzz stick with your jackknife from a piece of dry center wood. It will light from your match.
4. The lower dead branches of a pine tree will dry before the wood on the ground.
5. Take along trench candles. These are made from strips of newspaper, rolled and soaked in paraffin. These and old candle stubs make good fire-starters.
6. Waterproof your matches by dipping them in paraffin or coating the heads with nail polish. You may want to purchase a waterproof match container for your matches.

Putting out fires. Put out a fire as soon as you are finished using it. Scatter the logs; stir the ashes. Sprinkle it with water. Stir and sprinkle again. Bury it in sand or clay. You can be sure it is out if you can touch the spot with your bare hands.

After your fire is out always bury your ashes, and leave no sign of the fire. If sod was removed to build your fire, replace it so that your fire site is in as good or better condition than when you arrived.

Safety hints. Here are some safety hints to keep in mind when building fires:

1. Do not build a fire alone.
2. Do not permit campers to play with fire.
3. Break all used matches before throwing them away.
4. Have fire-fighting equipment on hand before striking that match.
5. If a fire gets out of hand, get help. Do not attempt to put it out unless you are *absolutely sure* you can extinguish it.
6. Don't try to outrun a fire, or run up a hill in front of one.
7. If you do attempt to fight a fire, keep the wind in your face.

Outdoor Cooking

In John 21 there is an account of a breakfast cookout which Christ and His disciples shared. The disciples had gone fishing, and when they got to land, Jesus had a fire of coals burning. We don't know whether it was started with a tepee, but we do know it was the right kind of a fire to bake fish, for it was a fire of coals!

Menu-planning. One of the first questions campers ask is: "What will we eat?" Good food helps make a good trip. Some camp leaders save their steaks and other best cuts of meat for trips. Gone are the days when a typical cookout consisted of a coffeepot on the fire and a dinner of cold baked beans eaten out of a can. Campers should eat as well on a cookout as they do back at camp, or perhaps better because they can try different fancy menus. They may even want to eat more, because eating outdoors actually seems to stimulate one's appetite.

Trip meals should be balanced and include some meat or other protein, milk, vegetables (green and yellow), salad or fruit, beverage, dessert, and a bread or cereal. In planning menus keep in mind the following factors:

Balance—Are your campers getting a balanced diet?

Amount—How many are going and how many meals will be eaten out? How much food is needed?

Perishability—How long will this food keep? Fresh milk and meats must be eaten soon. Canned or smoked meats, dehydrated food packets, and powdered food will keep. Dehydrated or freeze-dried foods suitable for camping trips may be purchased in many camping and sports equipment stores and in the camping equipment section of many department stores. If you wish to buy large quantities of these foods, it may be less expensive to buy them through suppliers.

Many items that carry well are available in your supermarket: dehydrated soups, potatoes, milk, dried fruits, instant puddings, cake mixes, biscuit mixes that double for pancakes, and powdered fruit juices to name a few.

Packing—How can I carry these items? Peaches, grapes, and plums taste good, have food value, and will quench thirst on a hike. But have you ever tried to carry these bulky and heavy foods for any distance? Avoid chocolate that will melt, or pie that will crush.

Bulk—Is there enough food value in relation to the space this food will take and the weight it will add to the pack? Fresh grapefruit is good, but you probably won't want to climb a mountain with several grapefruit in your pack. Whole potatoes will also be deleted when weight is a factor.

Cost—You may like filet mignon, but this is probably too expensive for your camp's budget. As a rule it costs more to feed a group out of camp than in the dining room. Though you'll figure on spending a little more, probably some items won't be bought because of their high costs.

What kinds of outdoor menus can be planned? Here are some ideas:

Sandwiches—For a short hike a bag lunch, candy, fruit, and sandwiches will suffice. Each camper carries his own, and this involves no cooking.

Picnic style lunches—This includes cold cuts, potato salad or some other salad, tomatoes, fruit, and Kool-Aid. This may be an outdoor Sunday night supper for your cabin or the whole camp. No cooking is needed.

Stick cookery—Often the first cooking tried by your campers will be done on a green stick.

Marshmallows should be toasted brown over coals, not burned black. (If campers lick off the powdered sugar first, this decreases the tendency to burn.)

Dilly dogs are hot dogs with wedges of cheese in them, wrapped with bacon. Thorns from a hawthorn tree, or small twigs, serve as toothpicks to hold the bacon in place.

Kabobs come in many varieties. Ingredients that have been used include beef, ham, bacon, carrots, potatoes, cheese, onions, peppers, tomatoes, seafood, and lamb. Numerous combinations of these (try your own) can be cooked on a stick over your coals. If you like meat rare, push the pieces close together; if you prefer yours well done, separate the pieces on your stick. For this type of stick cookery use a smooth, green stick about pencil-thickness. Clean the end and put a point on it with your jackknife.

Pigs in a blanket are sausages partially cooked on a stick, then covered with dough (Bisquick or similar mix) and returned to the fire. When finished, your cooked sausage is already in its own roll.

When cooking hot dogs or sausages on a stick, insert the stick on an angle through the food. If you put the stick through the end, or straight through the middle, the meat can easily fall off.

Pioneer drumsticks are made on sticks the thickness of a broomstick. Coat the end of your stick with a thin layer of hamburger, and cook over coals, not a flame. (Adding egg gives adhesiveness.) When finished, slide meat off the stick. Fill the hole with relish, mustard, or catsup and eat it in a roll.

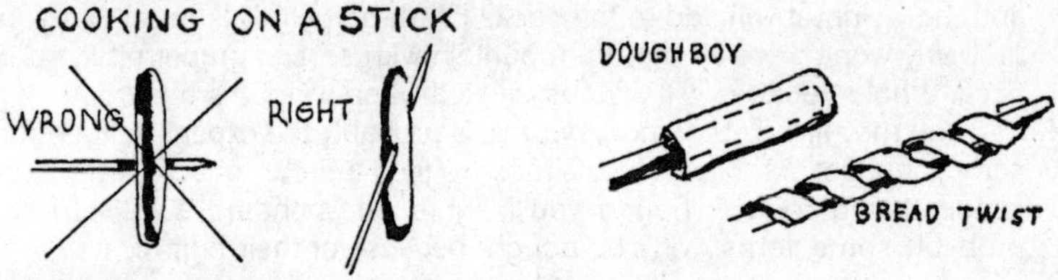

Doughboys also are made on a thick stick. Dough or biscuit mix can be prepared right in its box. Simply add a few spoonfuls of water, stir with a stick, and pick out your ball of dough. You can hand the box to the next camper. The dough will have the right consistency, and no mixing bowl is needed. (A plastic bag also may be used to mix dough, pancake mix, etc.). Spread the dough evenly in a thin coat on the stick. Be sure there are no holes in it. Toast over hot coals, turning so it will not burn. It should slide off the stick easily when finished. The hole may be filled with jelly. A variation of this is the *bread twist* on a stick, in which the dough is wrapped around the stick.

Aluminum foil cookery—Chicken, steak, fish, ham, bananas, biscuits, corn, vegetables, apples, and many other items can be cooked in foil. *Foil dinners* of hamburger, onion, potatoes, and carrots are a favorite. (Do not put any foil packet in a direct flame. Turn food over once during the cooking process. Foil dinners take 10-20 minutes cooking time, depending on how hot your fire is.) *Pinechams* of pineapple, cheese and ham are tasty. Baked apples with cinnamon, marshmallows, and brown sugar make a delicious dessert. *Banana boats* are made by stripping back one piece of banana skin and scooping out a bit of banana. Fill the space with chocolate and marshmallow. Put back the peel and wrap in foil. Leave in the coals only a few minutes, to melt the chocolate and marshmallow. Use a large piece of foil—never skimp.

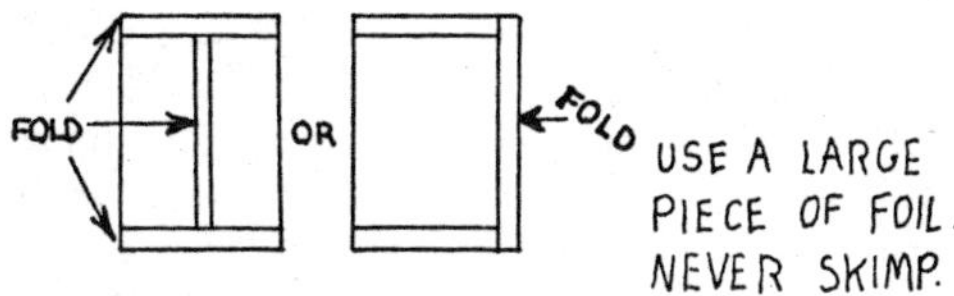

One-pot meals—Stews, soups, chicken and rice, hamburger, beef, tomatoes, corn, beans, peas, dumplings, cheese, and numerous combinations of these may be the ingredients of Indian stew, jungle stew, and casseroles.

Tin-can cookery—Into a one-pound coffee can, put hamburger, sliced potatoes and carrots, salt and pepper, onion if you wish, and ½ cup of water. Punch a few holes in the lid before replacing it. Bury the can in the coals. Provide one can per camper.

Hobo stoves may be made from No. 10 cans. Hammer the unopened top of the can slightly to make it concave, to better hold food. Cut a door approximately 5 inches wide by 3 or 4 inches high at the open bottom of the can. Punch holes with a can opener at the back of the can, near the top, to let the smoke out and to give a draft. Dig a trench under the can or support it on small stones to give more draft. Build your cooking fire under the can and cook on top of it, making sure the can is level. Bacon strips will grease the cooking surface. Eggs may be fried or scrambled on top of the can. If you like toast with your eggs, toast the bread by removing a piece from the center of the slice, and break an egg into this hole in the toast. When cooked, you will have eggs and bread cooked together. (Pancakes, hamburgers, and French toast can also be cooked on your hobo stove.)

Buddy burners, made from converted sardine cans or coffee cans, furnish good portable fuel for your hobo stove, for cooking in wet weather, or when other fuels are not available. A buddy burner may be made by filling your can with corrugated cardboard, cut to the can's height and coiled inside. After the cardboard is inserted, pour in melted paraffin until the can is full. This self-contained fuel burner may last for several meals.

Reflector-oven baking—Biscuits, pies, and cakes can be made outdoors by using a reflector oven, or a flat surface facing a reflector fire. A pan propped against a rock will also do for baking. A large oven can be made from half an oil drum. Make a shelf from the side removed from the drum. Fish may be planked on a board or log, and baked with heat reflected from a fire.

Barbecue—Roasts, chicken, duck, or a small pig may be cooked on a spit over a fire.

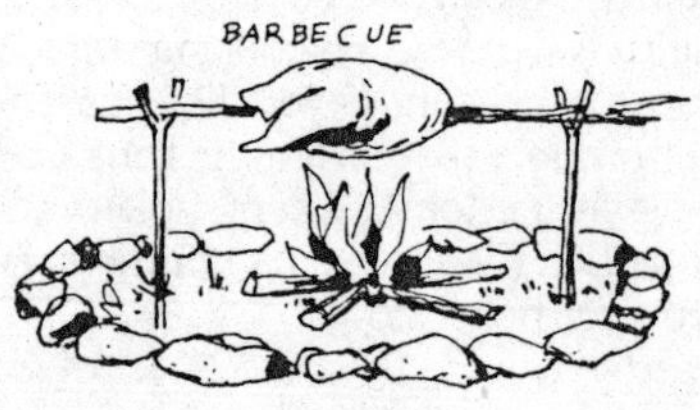

Bean-hole or *emu cooking* involves steaming food underground. Line the hole with hot rocks and put in your pot of meat, vegetables, ears of corn, or one-pot meal. Pack hot coals underneath, on top, and all around your pot of food. Cover with dirt or sod or a tarp and dirt. Allow food to cook slowly—6 to 8 hours or more.

Most inexperienced campers, do not take the time to cook their food thoroughly. Allow plenty of time to cook when outdoors. Teach your campers to wait until the food is properly cooked.

Easy desserts and salads:

S'mores—Each camper has two small squares of chocolate, two marshmallows, and two graham crackers. Toast marshmallows. Put chocolate on the graham crackers. Cover with toasted marshmallows and top with the second graham cracker. Squeeze it together and eat.

Robinson Crusoe—These are similar to s'mores, but peanut butter is substituted for chocolate.

Baked apples—Wrap in foil with marshmallows and cinnamon substituted for the core.

Mock angel food cake—Dip cubes of unsliced bread in condensed milk and roll them in coconut. Toast over coals. It tastes just like cake.

Stuffed celery—Clean celery and fill it with peanut butter or a cheese spread.

Walking salad—Core apples and fill the holes with cottage cheese and raisins or nuts.

Carrot sticks are easy to fix and eat on the trail.

Special Cooking Gadgets

Your campers will enjoy making special equipment for outdoor cooking. A *green-stick broiler* can be made from a forked green stick by bending one end around and weaving green twigs in and out until it resembles a tennis racket. Bread, hamburger, and hot dogs may be toasted or roasted on this green-stick broiler.

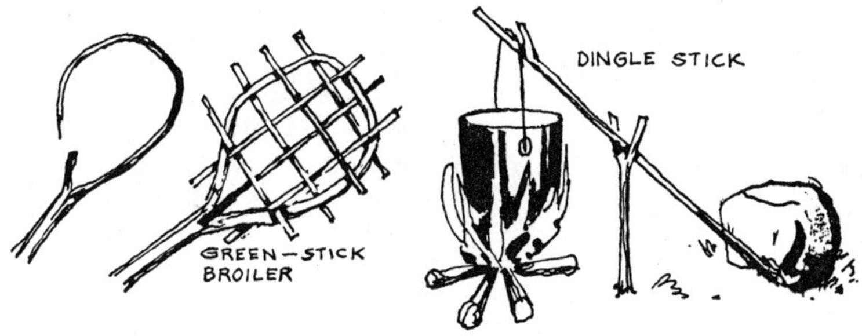

A *dingle stick* may be used to hold pots over a fire. Notch the stick, so your pot won't slip.

A *mixer* can be simulated by rubbing a forked stick between the hands.

Fish or corn can be *steam-cooked* in a wet newspaper or paper bag in coals.

A *double boiler* can be made with two sizes of tin cans. Put several small stones in water in the larger can; set the smaller can on these stones.

Eggs can be cooked on a hot flat rock. Is the rock sterile enough to cook on? It is, if it is hot enough to cook eggs.

Eggs may be baked by making a small hole in the pointed end of the egg before placing it in the coals.

Eggs taste good when cooked in an orange skin. Cut an orange in half. Eat the orange carefully, so the skin is not broken. Then break the egg into half of the orange skin and cook it in the coals.

Notched sticks will hold pots on a crane.

If you soap the outside of your pots before putting them over an open fire, they will be much easier to clean.

Some helpful measurements for outdoor cooking:

1 fistful = ¼ cup for a woman or ½ cup for a man
A 2-finger pinch = ⅛ teaspoon
A 3-finger pinch = ⅓ teaspoon
A 4-finger pinch = 1 teaspoon

To tell the temperature of your fire, hold your hand where you will place your food. Count one chimpanzee, two chimpanzees, etc. until you must remove your hand. A slow fire is 250-325° or six to eight chimpanzees. A medium fire is 325-

400° and four or five chimpanzees. Hot fires are 400-500° and two or three furry friends. A very hot fire is over 500°; no more than one chimpanzee can stand that heat.

Instant pudding poured into a pie crust of crumbled cookies makes a good pie.

Buffalo steaks are steaks laid right on the coals. Turn once. Brush off any embers and dip the steaks in melted butter. Edible? You've never tasted anything better!

Potatoes can be rolled into the coals without foil, or you may bake them in wet sand in a No. 10 can that's buried in coals.

Storing food

In warm weather a cache underground will keep food cooler than above ground. If you are near water, a well of stones built in the water will help keep perishables that are encased in plastic containers or milk cartons. (Be sure to place your food in the shade.) Nonperishables may be hung from a tree. A tin can on your rope will keep squirrels from helping themselves to your breakfast. Or a watertight container fastened to a tree branch overhanging the lake or stream that allows the food to be in the water will keep things cool.

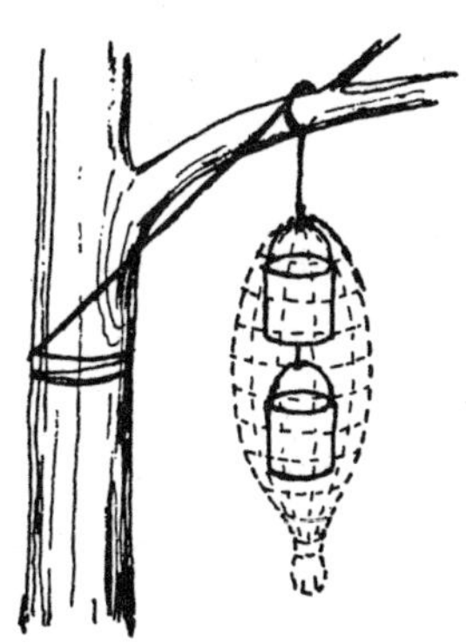

A good cache above ground, which will keep your food cool and free from animals and insects, depends on the principle of evaporation.

Tie two buckets or tin cans together, one over the other. Place your food in the bottom bucket and water in top bucket. Weight down a piece of thin cloth or cheesecloth with a stone in the upper water bucket and tie it down underneath the bottom bucket of food.

13
More Camping Skills

Camp Ax, Saw, and Knife

In order to make a good woodpile and fire, your campers must learn the correct uses of the tools of outdoor living. One basic camp tool is the camp ax. Always keep your camp ax sharp. A dull ax can be more dangerous than a sharp one. Keep the handle tight. Use a wedge to tighten a loose handle (the wooden handle will tighten temporarily if soaked in water).

Carry your short ax in its sheath. If worn on the belt, it should hang on the back of the hip, blade facing away from the body. Keep it sharpened with a file or stone. Run the file across the blade in a circular motion toward the heel of the head. Never use an ax or knife to stir a fire or you will destroy its temper.

Practice safety at all times. When passing an ax to some-

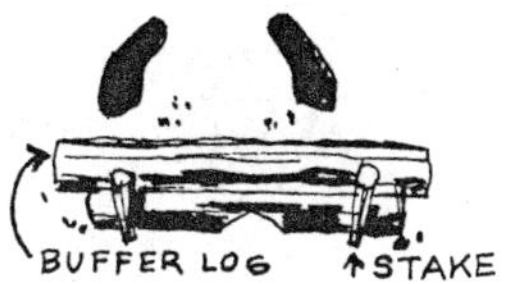

one, hold it by the handle with the blade toward you. Do not let go until the receiver has a grip on the ax and says "Thank you" to indicate he has the tool. When using a camp ax, stand with feet apart, so that in swinging, the ax's arc will be between your legs. Use another log as a buffer between you and the log you are chopping. Before you start, swing the ax slowly in all directions. This arc of safety should be clear of underbrush, overhanging branches, and other obstacles. The nearest person should be at least twice this distance from you.

Use a chopping block for small wood. Chop with even strokes.

Cut halfway into a log with V-cuts, then roll the log over and chop V-cuts on the other side.

In lopping off tree branches, stand on the opposite side from which you are chopping and chop upward, toward the top of the tree.

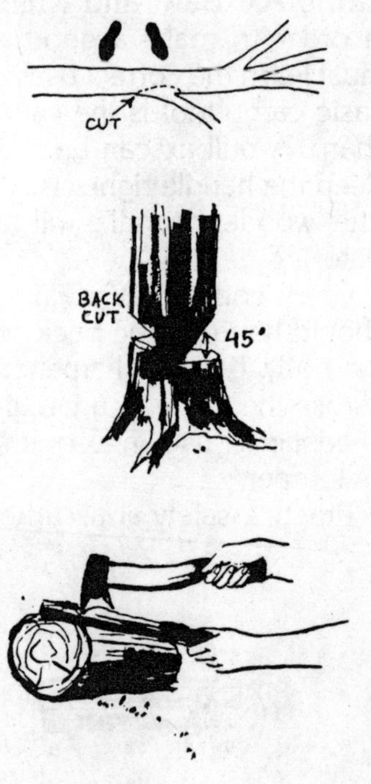

When a piece of wood you are splitting gets stuck to your ax, raise both and hit your chopping block.

To cut a small, live sapling, bend it at the ground level and cut it close to the ground.

Before cutting down a tree (never cut a tree needlessly) be sure you first secure the owner's permission. Then line up your ax with the tree, to see which way it is leaning. Clear the area around the tree before cutting. Make a 45° cut on the side you want the tree to fall; then make a higher back cut. As the tree falls, stand to one side of it, not behind it.

For safety's sake store your camp ax in its sheath. Or sink its cutting edge into a stump or log, making sure that the handle does not extend over the edge.

Always rest when you are tired. It is easy to lose control of your tools when muscles are fatigued.

Saw

A favorite camp tool, especially with girls, is the small bow saw.

Keep the blade snug and allow the saw to glide easily through the cut. Do not try to saw above waist height, and use a saw horse or stump to support the wood you are sawing. For camp use there are small pocket wire saws, collapsible saws, and a lightweight bow saw. Two-man saws can be used for heavy timber.

Oil your saw before storing it, and keep the blade in a shield when not in use.

When you hand a saw to someone, pass it with the blade face down. Do not let go of it until he replies, "Thank you."

Knife

Perhaps most of your campers will bring jackknives to camp. At least some of them will need instruction in the proper use and care of a knife, to prevent injury and the carving of initials in camp buildings and furniture.

Always open the blade all the way, with two hands. Use two hands when closing the blade. Always cut away from you, and be careful to keep your thumb off the back of the blade when cutting.

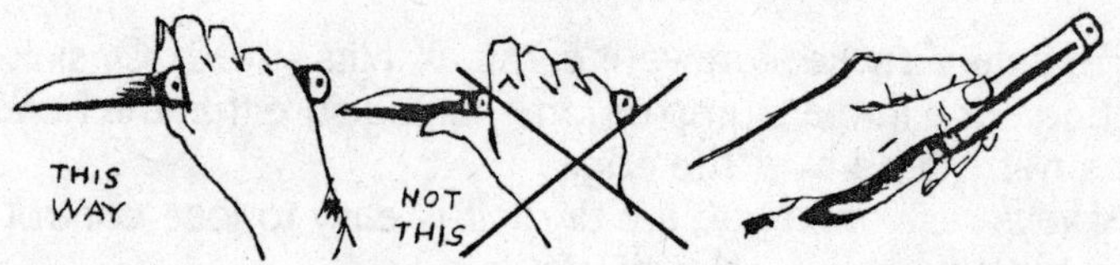

Keep your knife clean, oiled, and sharp. To sharpen, rotate the knife edge in a circular motion along a whetstone or carborundum stone. To pass a knife, either close it first, or hold it blade down and hand the handle to the receiver.

A hunting knife should be handled similarly to a jackknife and passed the same way. This knife is usually worn on a belt, on the back of the hip. Be sure that it fastens securely in its sheath.

Gear and Shelter

Your campers ask, "What shall we take on our trip?" This will be determined by how long you'll be gone, how you are going (via truck, foot, or canoe), and how you forecast the weather.

Gear may be divided into shared and personal equipment:

Personal gear may include: sturdy shoes, a jacket or sweater, two pairs of socks, long pants or jeans, poncho, swimsuit, towel, soap, washcloth, handkerchief, Chapstick, brush and comb, toothpaste and toothbrush, change of underwear, and perhaps a sun hat, shorts, and shirt. The tendency is to take too much. Lay out what you think you will need. Then, before going on the trip, try limiting yourself to these articles for a couple days. You may find you have forgotten some items and there will probably be some things that you didn't use at all. You may leave these latter items at camp. Don't forget your Bible or Testament, a notebook and pencil, sunglasses, and maybe your camera. A harmonica, guitar, or uke would add much to your singing around the fire. You will need a sleeping bag or bedroll, a knapsack or backpack for carrying your things if you are hiking, flashlight, drinking cup, knife, fork, and spoon (or mess kit), jackknife, and possibly a canteen and a large red bandana.

Shared equipment would include: shelter (tarp, tent, tube tent, or sheet of plastic), food and cooking equipment, first-aid kit, toilet paper, bug repellent, waterproof matches, camp ax and/or saw, shovel, dish towel, scouring pad, sponge and soap for washing pots, map, and compass. Include some rope, and a file or sharpening stone for keeping tools sharp. More equipment will be needed for longer trips. Someone in your group should have a watch and some money for emergency phone calls. Candles or gadgets to help start a fire in wet weather are helpful and some pocket-size books for games and wildlife identification will be useful. Repair kits for canoe or bicycle (if you are going that way), and a whistle for emergencies may come in handy and won't add that much weight to your pack.

Packing

Pack all of your personal gear, except eating utensils, in your sleeping bag. If you do not have a sleeping bag, roll your blankets into a bedroll, after putting your personal gear inside. Tie the bedroll securely. If you will be hiking without packs you can bend your bedroll into a horseshoe pack. Instead of rolling it up from foot to top, roll it from side to side. This can be worn over a shoulder, which leaves your hands free for climbing. (A horseshoe pack can also be tied over your backpack.)

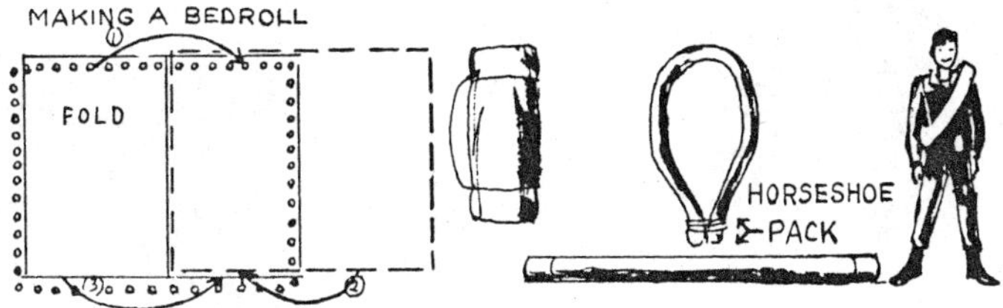

Plastic bags, ditty bags, and drawstring bags are useful for packing personal items. Food packed by meals avoids having to empty your whole pack each time you stop.

A laundry bag or pillow case serves as a pack for a short hike. Tie stones in the corners to hold the rope. Spare trousers can also be made into a pack.

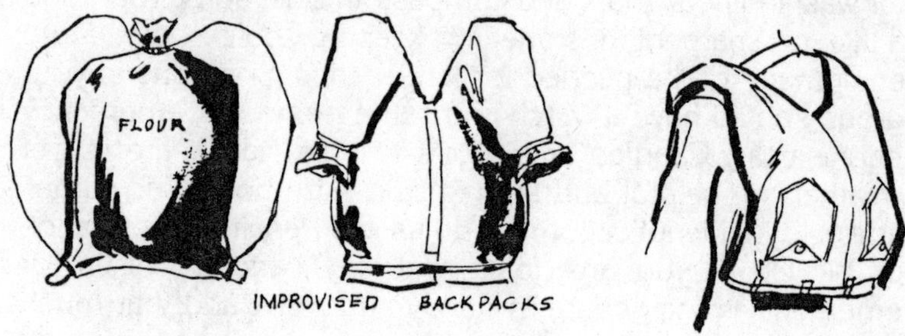

In packing the duffel you'll carry on your back, put heavy things on top. Your pack should ride high. Packboards, pack baskets, and Yucca packs all are widely used. The aluminum frame and rucksack, which ride easily, are favorites of mountain climbers. Indians used a tumpline around the head to relieve some of the weight from their shoulders.

A waterproof duffel bag is good for canoe-tripping. Pack your blanket in the front of your pack, next to your back. Group all articles for easy access. Keep your poncho near the top, in case of rain; and your first-aid kit in an outside pocket, so it may be reached in a hurry.

Sleeping Out

Slip your poncho or ground cloth under your sleeping bag, unless your bag is waterproofed underneath. The secret of keeping warm when sleeping out is to put as many layers under you as over you, to help retain your body heat. A hooded sweat shirt will keep your head and shoulders warm. An extra pair of woolen socks will warm your feet. Don't sleep in the same clothes that you have been wearing during the day.

Remove all roots, rocks, and bumps before putting down your sleeping bag. (For comfort's sake you may scoop out dirt where your hips and shoulders lie.) An air mattress or foam pad adds to one's comfort, but also to the weight of one's pack.

A comfortable bed can be made with an extra blanket. Fold the blanket over two poles. Lash the poles to two logs.

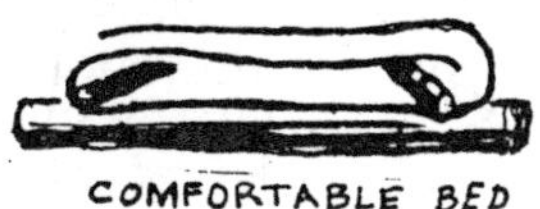

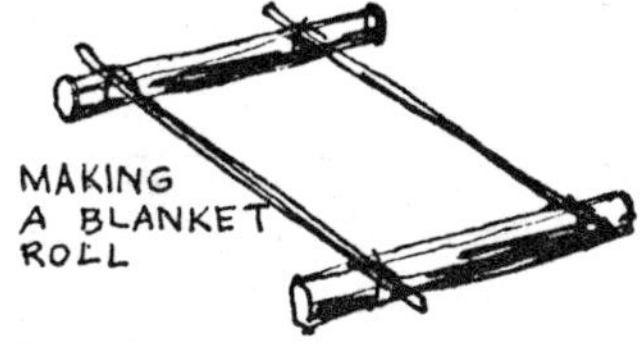

Shelter

If you do not have to carry your gear (as in wagon or car camping), a heavier tent with floor and poles is desirable. But for tripping by canoe or backpacking, this type of tent is too heavy. A lightweight cloth tent or a tarpaulin saves space and weight. (If the weather is good, you may enjoy sleeping out on the ground with no shelter. However, when away from camp, it is wise to take along shelter to be prepared for bad weather.) An inexpensive 9-by-12-foot plastic drop cloth makes a temporary waterproof shelter when stretched over a rope and weighted down with rocks along the edges.

A tarp can be tied between trees with a rope, or supported

with lashed sticks. A *canoe shelter* will be protection for three or four persons, depending on the tarp's size. A *pyramid* or *forester tent* gives more protection from cold and rain. Tent poles may be made from saplings, or your tent may be tied up to an overhanging tree branch. A tarp may be folded to make either of these tents.

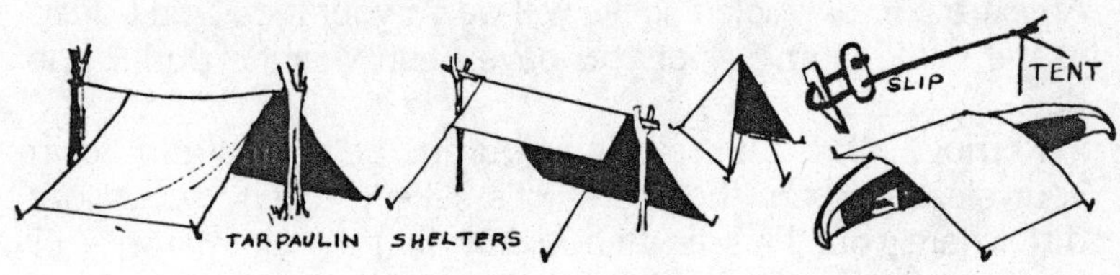

Pitch your tent so that it is neat and tight. (You *pitch* a tent when you put it up and *strike* it when you take it down.) A tautline hitch or two half hitches can be used to fasten tent ropes. Set your rope at a 90° angle to the tent. Always loosen ropes when they are wet, as they shrink and may rip your tent (unless you use synthetic rope which does not shrink). Slips may be used to tighten or loosen ropes quickly.

In soft ground or sand you may need two pegs per rope to secure your tent.

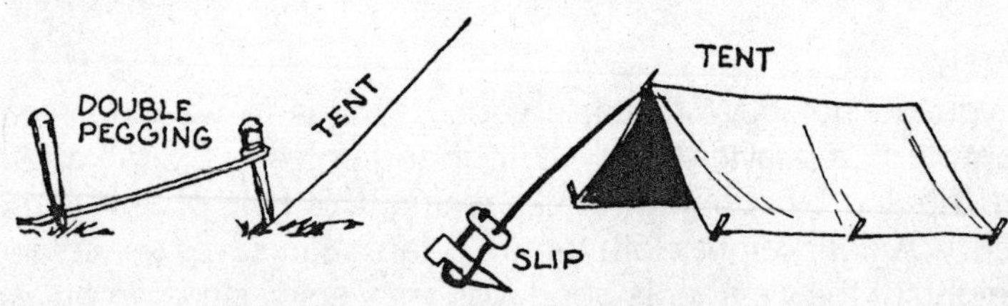

Do not touch the inside of a tent in the rain unless you want a leaky tent. If you do have a leak, a string pinned to the leak may guide the drops down the string line and away from your bed.

In sand, where tent pegs will not hold, a "dead man" may be used. This is made by tying two crossed sticks or logs together and fastening your tent ropes to them. Bury each anchor in a foot or more of sand.

If you expect rain, dig a ditch around your tent to carry away ground water and to keep the rain from running down the sides and underneath your tent. Channel the water away from your tent at the lowest spot.

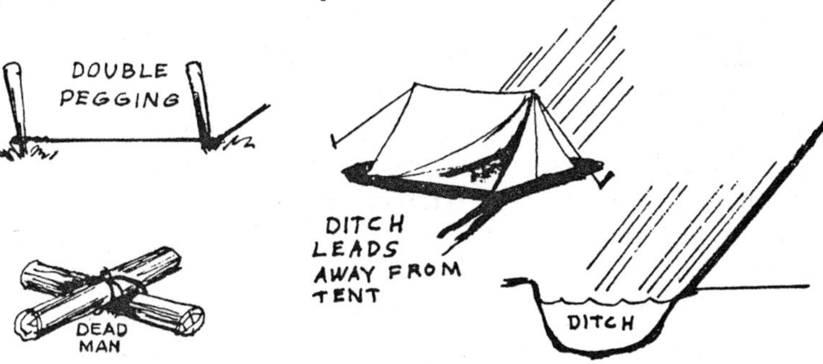

Sanitation

A good camper is a clean camper. Put a pail of water on your fire before supper, to have hot water for dishes. Rinse dishes in very hot water. Enjoy the comfort of washing yourself with hot water.

If you are traveling light, dishes may be washed in ponchos or plastic bags. Dig two holes in the ground and line them with your ponchos or plastic bags. One hole is for washing, the other for rinsing. You may take along scouring pads, but sand or bed-straw plants also work well for scouring.

Drinking water should always be purified on a trip, unless you are absolutely sure it is safe. Water may be boiled for 20 minutes to sterilize it, and then aerated by pouring it from one container to another.

Halizone tablets, available from your drugstore, will purify water.

Burn and bury your garbage deep enough so that small animals will not dig it up. Tin cans should be burned and flattened before you bury them or carry them out with you.

For personal sanitation, dig your latrine at least 100 yards away from camp. A straddle type—one foot wide and more than a foot deep—is the easiest to make. Leave the pile of dirt and shovel beside it. A rack for toilet paper may be made from a forked stick. The paper may be covered with a plastic bag or a tin can to keep it dry.

Knots

There are at least 8,296 knots. You won't need all of these, but learn a few useful ones for camp. You will need them to tie your bedroll, to secure your tent, and to lash camp equipment. Knots consist of hitches, bends, bights, loops, and combinations of these. Learn the use of several knots, to recognize them by sight, and to tie them in the dark. A good knot will tie easily, hold fast, will not jam, and will untie easily.

To keep a rope from fraying, tie a knot near its end, or wrap the end tightly with tape. Synthetic ropes may be melted on the ends with a match. Or you may *whip* the end of your rope.

To do this, take a piece of string about 12 inches long and loop it along the end of your rope. Hold this loop of string with your thumb and forefinger and start winding the string around your rope. When you have wound about an inch, tuck your end through the loop you made in the beginning. Pull the short end of string, which will pull the loop and other end under the wrapping. Cut off both ends close to the winding. It should be tight enough so you can't pull it off.

A *square knot* is used to join two ends of rope, tie a bandage, fix a shoestring, or to tie two pieces of rope together. Follow the diagram for a square knot.

A *sheet bend* is another joining knot. It is useful because it joins ropes of different thicknesses when other knots permit slipping.

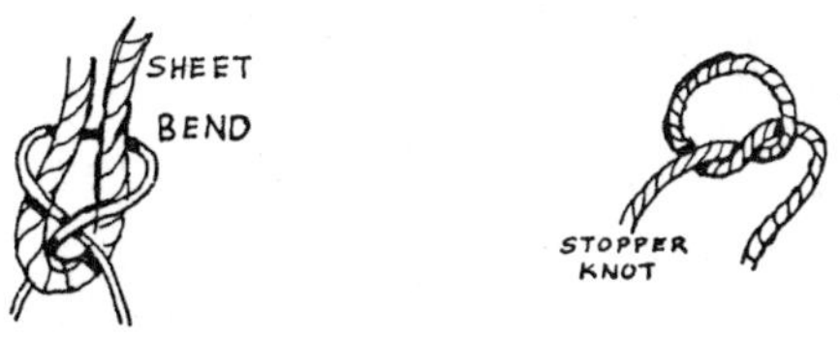

A *stopper knot,* which will prevent a rope from slipping through a grommet, is useful. The simplest of these is the *overhand.* This knot can also be used to keep your rope from raveling.

A *bowline knot* will form a permanent loop that will not slip on the end of a rope. It may be used to pull a camper up a cliff or to bring him in to shore from the water. It is useful any time you need a nonslip loop.

Two *half hitches* will hold rope lines to a tree or fasten your clothesline.

The *clove hitch* is used to tie boats to a dock, and in lashing projects.

A *tautline hitch* is used to tie guy lines to tent pegs. Your lines can be tightened or slackened by pushing the knot up or down.

No knot is as strong as the original rope. A permanent, as well as stronger, way to connect two ends of rope is to *splice* them. In a splice the rope strands are woven into each other. An *eye splice* makes a loop on the end of a rope. A *long splice* and a *short splice* weave two ropes together to make a longer rope. A *ring splice* makes a circle of rope.

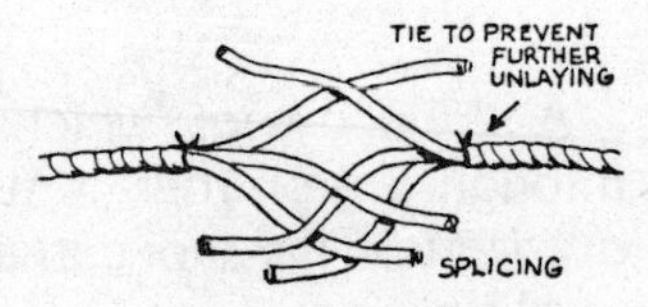

Lashing

You can spend profitable hours with your campers making lashed camp equipment.

Square lashing is a useful method for fastening two sticks or poles together. Start with a clove hitch and wrap your rope or lashing twine over and under several times. The secret of tight lashing is *frapping.* This is done by wrapping your rope around the lashing but between the sticks.

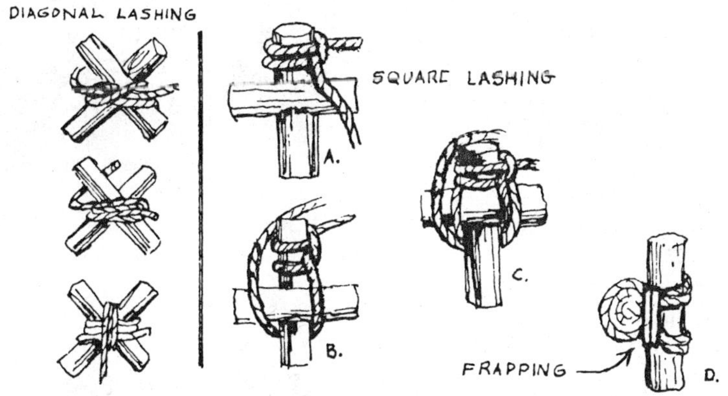

Diagonal lashing is done in a similar way to square lashing, except that your ropes cross the intersection instead of going under and over and around it.

Sheer lashing will extend the length of a pole. It may be handy for the ridge pole of your tent. Sheer lashing may also be used in putting together a tripod.

Continuous lashing, when many short sticks are fastened to one or more long ones, is used to make tabletops, beds, chairs, and benches. Begin at the end of your long pole and the middle of your rope with a clove hitch. Pull your ropes from this knot over your first small stick, then down back of your big stick, and cross your ropes before bringing them forward and over your second small stick (see sketches).

Once you know lashing you'll be able to make shoe racks,

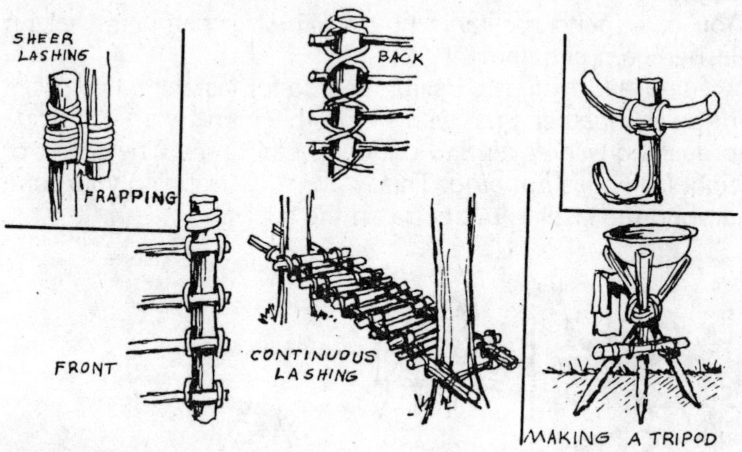

coat hangers, tree houses, tables, beds, and numerous other things.

Finding Your Way

The sun "rises"in the east and "sets" in the west. So if the sun is on your right in the morning, you are facing north. If the setting sun is on your right, you are facing south.

You can tell your direction more accurately if you have a watch (and the sun is out). Hold a stick perpendicular to the center of your watch. Turn the watch around until the shadow of the stick covers the hour hand. Halfway between 12 and the hour (whichever way makes the smallest angle) will be due

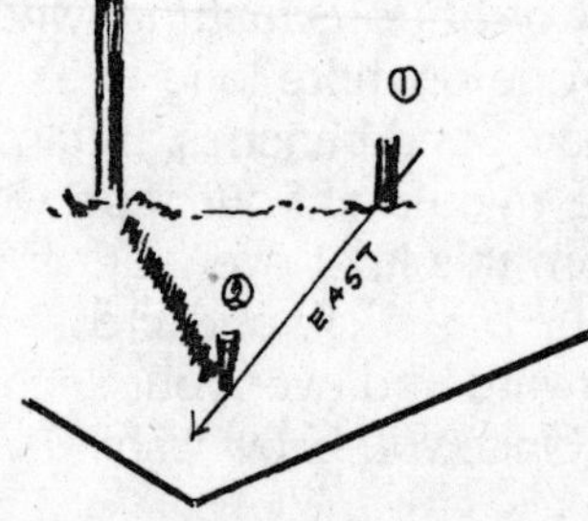

north. (Be sure your watch is running and is close to the correct time. Adjust for Daylight Saving Time.)

Another way to determine direction is to drive a stick into the ground. Mark the top of the stick's shadow. Sit down and wait until the shadow moves. Mark the top of the shadow again. Draw a straight line from your first mark to your second mark. This will be east.

At night you will be able to tell north by the position of the Big Dipper. Follow the pointers, the two outer stars of the Dipper's cup. The star in line with these is Polaris, the North Star. After a few nights sleeping out under the stars, you can learn to tell time by the position of the Dipper in the sky. All of the stars rotate around Polaris. The Dipper changes position through the night but it always points to the North Star.

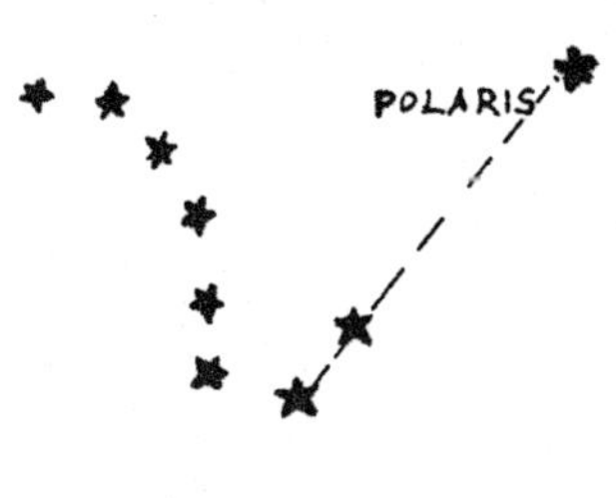

Map and Compass

As a good camper, however, you will have with you a magnetic compass, so you won't get lost.

The simplest compass is a free-moving needle on a bearing. An induction-dampened or liquid-filled compass is steadier, but also more expensive. In the lensatic compass the entire dial rotates to give a quick reading.

When you use your compass, hold it level in your hand and stay clear of overhead wires, electrical fences, and any electrical disturbance which might influence your compass. A compass is oriented when the free-moving needle comes to rest over the "N" point. Turn the compass around until the needle points to "N." East will be 90° and south will be 180°.

On a compass hike you may be given a reading of "30°, 50 feet." You orient your compass to north, find 30°, sight some object along your 30° line, then pace 50 feet toward that object. If you do this accurately, you will come to your next marker.

On this kind of hike, a Silva compass, which combines a protractor and a compass, is often used. With the Silva compass follow a bearing by setting the compass for your reading by the direction-of-travel arrow in front of you, and turn around till the needle is oriented to north. Find a landmark and walk toward it.

To lay a compass trail, reverse this procedure. Sight your object. Orient your compass and take a reading to it. Campers enjoy laying and following compass hikes and trails.

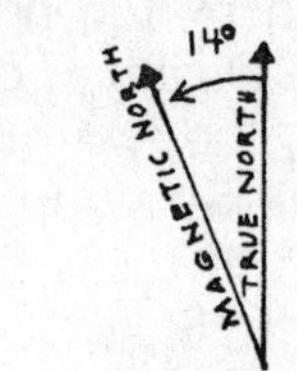

Unfortunately, true north and magnetic north are not exactly the same. Your compass points to a spot some 1,400 miles south of the north pole. If you live in the East, your reading will be too low. In the West your reading will be too high. This angle of variation is called declination, and you should compensate your compass reading to correct this. The number of degrees of declination will be indicated at the bottom of your topographical map. (This makes no difference on a compass hike, but it does affect map and compass work.) By adding or subtracting the number of degrees of declination in your area, you get an accurate reading.

On some compasses you can set the dial for the degree of error and get correct readings each time. Add degrees in the East; subtract them in the West. Many hikes and games can be played with a compass alone. Add a topographical map and you have a map and compass activity (cross-country trip and exploration) with which to challenge advanced campers.

A map is a reproduction of the earth's surface. It's like an airplane view—in fact, most maps are made from aerial photographs. A good topographical map gives you a great amount of detail. Every house, building, lake, stream, water-

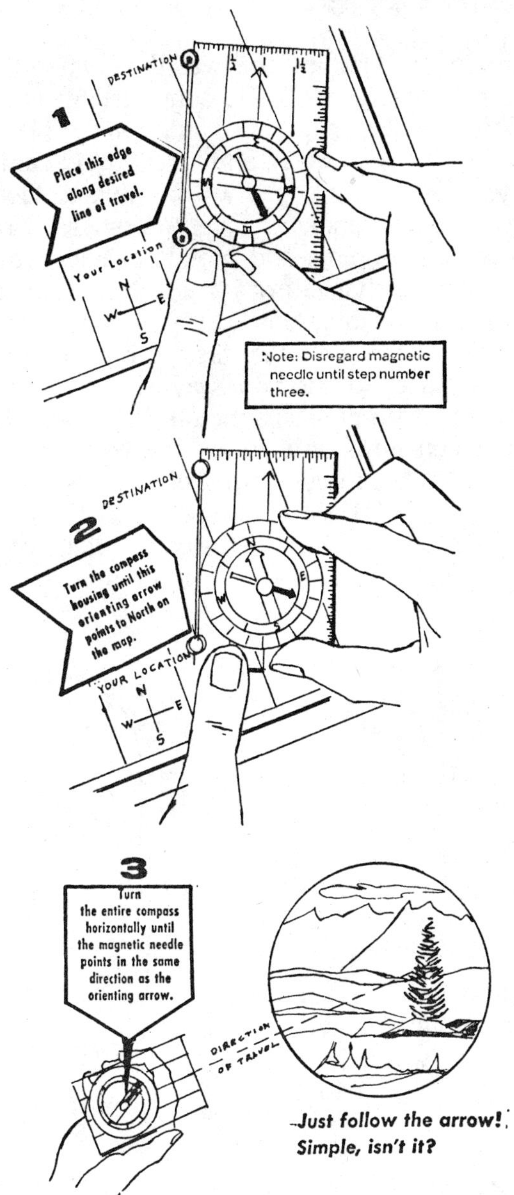

Just follow the arrow! Simple, isn't it?

fall, footpath, and orchard that was there when the map was made may be designated. The contour lines mark elevation levels. From such a map your campers can plan overnights and trips by foot or by water, and locate good camping areas. Before you leave camp, you will be able to locate springs, overnight shelters, drinking water, marshes, railroads, high-level areas for camping, and mountain trails. Topographical maps can be purchased from the U.S. Department of Geological Survey, Washington, D.C. 20025. You may want to send for a map index circular first, to locate the section you wish to purchase. To find your way with map and compass, follow the three simple steps pictured on page 185.

If your watch stops on a sunny day, you can tell time with your compass. Hold your compass in the sun and turn the housing until the "S" is under the magnetic needle. Hold a small stick or pencil upright in the center of the compass. The shadow will indicate the bearing of the sun. You can tell the approximate time by the chart below.

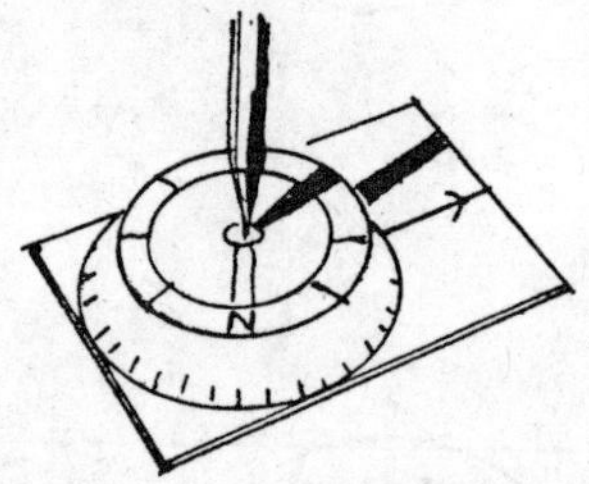

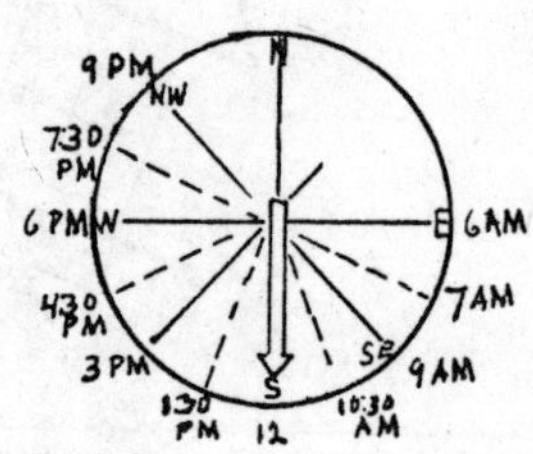

Trail Signs

Trail signs are the street signs of the forest. When you enter the woods, mark your path every 30 to 50 yards so you can find your way back again. Do not mark trees with an ax or remove bark, as this damages

Here are tied grass signals.

them. Sometimes the state fastens a trail marker to a tree to guide you. When your group is laying its own trail or making a trail for another cabin to follow, leave some of the woodsman's trail signs.

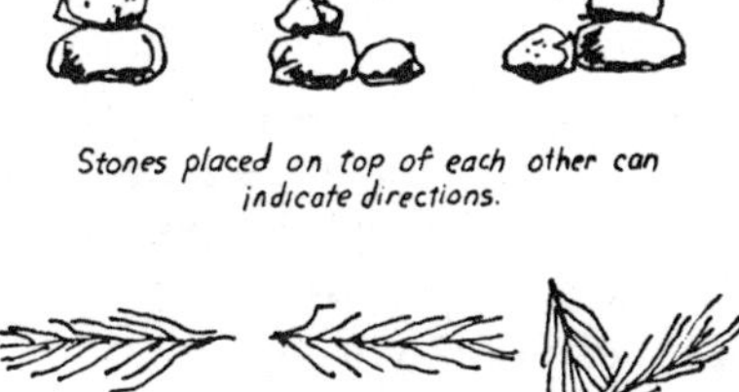

Stones placed on top of each other can indicate directions.

So can twigs along the path.

A twig bent over means you are on the right trail. A twig lying on the path means the path goes in the direction of the broken end. An arrow scratched in the path or made with sticks will also give direction.

Three of anything—three shots, three whistles, three stones, or three knotted grasses—means danger, look out, or help. Two or three smokey fires, close together, also mean help.

Mark your trails clearly. The point is to help those who follow you and perhaps to help yourself.

If lost, and you never should be if you mark your trail and carry your compass, do not wander aimlessly around or wear yourself out running. Sit down. Think where you saw your last marker or last familiar object. Plan what to do. It's usually best to go downhill. You will probably come to a stream. This will flow down to a larger stream or river and to civilization. Listen for sounds of cars on highways. Look for the position of the sun overhead or the location of the Big Dipper. Remember which direction you came from camp. Follow a power line down a mountain. This may be steep, but it will be a shortcut down.

If you are on a road in a country area and you need to phone for help, follow the telephone lines to the nearest lead off the trunk line. It will lead you to a house with a phone.

If all attempts to orient yourself fail, plan to camp where you are and let someone find you. Make yourself comfortable. Keep busy gathering wood, gathering berries, and fixing yourself a safer shelter. This will help keep you from panicking.

If you are with a group of campers and stray off the trail, have the group stay together and sing loudly. This helps morale. If it's night, let them shine their flashlights. You and a camper spiral out around the group, to locate your last marker. As you circle around them, stay in sight of their lights or within earshot of their singing. When you find a familiar marker, call to them and bring them over to you. Repeat this process until you are on the path again or out of the woods.

Do not go into unfamiliar woods without your map and compass. Then you won't get lost. Be a good campcrafter!

Now that you're up on map and compass, knots and lashing, trail signs, fire-building, and other campcraft skills, the whole outdoors is your home. Enjoy it. Share it with your campers. Relax and feel at home in it. Our Lord "richly provides us with everything for our enjoyment" (1 Tim. 6:17).

14 Especially for Directors

Though this book is written primarily for counselors, it is meant to be used by you in training sessions before camp. Good counselors are needed for good camps, and good training is one of the most urgent needs of Christian camps today. Profitable camping depends more on first-rate leadership than on all your facilities, equipment, and programs put together.

You will need to adapt this material to your own camp's situation and needs. Select and stress that which relates to your camp.

Recruitment

Enlist your staff early. You may recruit from Sunday Schools, youth departments, the general church constituency, colleges, Bible schools, and by re-enlisting previous staff members. Some counselors are working people who give a week or more of vacation to counsel. Others are housewives. Public school teachers and other Christian professional people may be challenged by the opportunity to serve the Lord in this way.

Selecting Your Staff

The first contact with a new staff member may be through correspondence and your application form. (See the sample staff application form on p. 201.) If you don't know an applicant, you may also want two or three references.

When you receive the application, arrange for an interview, if at all possible. Attitudes and purposes can be explored in an interview, and this is the beginning of your rapport with a new staff member. The prospective counselor should also feel free to ask you questions. If you believe this person has a contribution to make to your camp, and if the applicant believes that your camp is a place where the Lord wants him to serve, you may have him sign an agreement. The agreement should state: the responsibilities of both the counselor and the camp (see p. 203 for sample agreement), dates when your counselor arrives at and leaves camp, remuneration and travel expenses (if any), days and hours off. It should also state the counselor's responsibility for attending your training sessions. You keep one copy of the signed agreement; your new counselor retains the other.

Out-of-camp Training

Begin training by mailing educational materials and letters of a challenging nature to your counselors. You may give reading assignments in camping books or you may advise prospective staff members to take college or Red Cross courses in first aid, life saving, or small craft. Notify your staff when and where these courses are taught in their areas. Christian Camping International (Box 646, Wheaton, Ill. 60189), and the American Camping Association (Bradford Woods, Martinsville, Ind. 46151) conduct conventions and workshops which help any of your staff members who can attend them. The CCI *Camping Journal* and the ACA's *Camping* magazine are well worth sending to your staff.

Send mailings regularly to your staff till camptime. A brochure with map and directions to your camp, a list of what to bring, and a job analysis detailing the counselor's responsibilities can also be sent in advance.

Any teaching materials—for Bible studies, quiet times, and cabin devotions—should be sent to staff members well in advance of camp so they may come adequately prepared. Once camp gets underway, there's not much time for study.

If a medical examination is required of staff (and it should be), this form should be sent too.

Also send each counselor any helpful materials related to activities he will be leading or assisting in. If he is leading archery, for example, he should know how many days a week and for how long a time each day he will be conducting archery class. It would help him to know what equipment will be available. He should then prepare his material and send you his lesson plans for the archery period. His plans should include alternate rainy day ideas and a list of the equipment he needs. You or your program director should check his lesson plans before camp.

In general, your training program should help each counselor to:

Be sure that he is walking close to the Lord, and to depend wholly on God to help him win and train his campers for Christ
Know the ins and outs of his job
Increase his understanding of being a leader of youth in a camp situation (including the importance of counseling individual campers)
Acquire or improve skills of outdoor living, and become acquainted with all activities of the camp program
Learn more about his camp's contribution to the development of its campers.
Understand staff relationships and responsibilities

Because counselors' applications come to you at different times, and because there is such a variety of material to be sent to each accepted applicant, you may want to keep a chart of your correspondence (see sample form, p. 200). This chart can also remind you to write those thank-you letters after camp.

To help your counselors keep their camp materials together, you may send each one a binder. When they get to camp, they can add more materials to this looseleaf book which becomes their counselor's manual. A completed counselors' manual may include:

- A special letter of welcome
- Words and music of the camp song and the camp theme song
- Map of your site
- Map or brochure of the area, showing places of interest
- Quiet-time suggestions
- Cabin devotional helps
- Dining room procedures
- Health center information
- Camp chore procedures
- Daily and Sunday schedules
- Schedule of special events and evening programs
- Letters of challenge
- List of camp policies
- Signed agreement, counselor's copy
- Job analysis
- Schedule of precamp training sessions and agenda
- Schedule of pre-in-camp training and agenda
- Instructor's Manual and Camper's Do-It Book, for Bible study
- Extra schedule sheets for own schedules
- Planning sheets for cabin activities
- Information about the camp's bank
- Camper evaluation forms
- Waterfront regulations
- Fire drill and evacuation procedures
- Sample caper chart (see p. 40)
- Other helpful information

Time spent training your staff is well spent. It pays dividends during the camping season. Even if you have to shorten the camping period a bit in order to train counselors on the site, it is worthwhile. If you cannot get into a rented site until Saturday, it is wise to train your staff on the weekend and start camp on Monday (unless you have a well-trained, veteran staff).

Precamp Training

If the staff members live near camp, precamp training may be conducted during the winter and spring months. While the snow still covers your camp road, you can cover the philosophy of your camp, its aims, history, traditions, policies, and organizational structure.

A counselor-training checklist is helpful in keeping a record of the training each of your staff members receives. If Jeanne has attended training sessions 1, 3, 4, and 5, and Paul has only been able to be at sessions 2, 3, and 4, the material covered in the missing sessions can be made up at camp after they arrive for pre-in-camp training.

The how of campcraft skills, cooking outdoors, and familiarization with nature can best be done in the spring, when the weather is warmer. It's preferable to do this on your own site, but a state park or forest preserve will suffice.

In camps where staff members come from great distances, most of the training is usually *in-camp* training, on the site. Some camps conduct a week or 10 days of training prior to the opening of camp. Regardless of where the winter precamp training is conducted, there should always be pre-in-camp training, as well as in-service (on-the-job) training. All counselors should report to camp at least 24 hours before the campers arrive. This pre-in-camp training time sets the tone and pace for all of camp. This is when the "where" and "what" of camping are covered. Your new staff members need to be oriented to the site. They should know where equipment is located, where each building and facility is, and where special spots for hikes, campfires, and overnights may be found. Dining hall procedures can be demonstrated at mealtime.

Make provision during pre-in-camp training for counselors to get to know each other, to work and plan together in small groups. Evening programs may be developed together by counselors who will be working with the same age-group. There may be areas of camp to get ready for the campers' coming, but care should be taken that this does not become a work period for the purpose of opening camp. The setting aside of one day to go through an entire day of camp is helpful to the staff. This should include the flag ceremony, Bible study, quiet time, dining hall traditions, rest hour, free-time activities, and evening cabin devotions. This affords counselors time to see camp in action and to learn by doing. An evening program should be demonstrated and some camp songs should also be learned.

Counselors should have the opportunity to visit all of the activities offered by the camp and to become somewhat acquainted with each one, so they can better interest their campers. For example, in a pre-in-camp training day a counselor goes to the rifle range. He is given the safety regulations and the class procedures for riflery. He is taught how to hold a rifle. He becomes familiar with the instructor's range commands: "Position! Load! Fire! Bolts open!" From here your counselor may go to the craft shop to learn what mediums of crafts are available and receive basic instructions in the use of tools. Perhaps he will have time to make some article.

Here is one overall plan for training counselors:

	Time	Content
Correspondence	Letters sent in the spring	1. On receipt of application send: welcome letter, counselor agreement, letter of challenge. 2. On receipt of signed agreement send: job analysis, second letter of challenge, list of books to read, Bible study material. 3. Send third letter of challenge, counselor training helps, cabin devotion helps, campfire message suggestions, health form.
Precamp training	Weekend	Discuss aims, doctrine, and philosophy of camp, psychology of campers, recommended bibliography, how to teach Bible studies, activity assignments, cabin assignments. Go over program in general.
Pre-in-camp training	1-10 days	Get to know each other; go through a daily schedule; develop evening programs; discuss health, morale, and safety; become familiar with site and environs; gain experience in nature, craft, and trip programs; make caper charts; note kitchen procedures; get experience in cooking out; discuss music in camp; teach camp songs; discuss enlarging aims and philosophy of camp program; prepare materials; get cabins ready; receive a spiritual challenge.
In-service training	30 minutes of counselor meetings each day; individual interviews and evaluations	Plan to cover more specific problems and weak points. Give help when difficulties arise; schedule regular interviews and evaluation sessions. Make spiritual challenge a part of every contact.

If a series of workshops is scheduled for winter and/or spring precamp training, they may cover the following:

First workshop:	Get-acquainted time Philosophy and aims History of your camp Games and sports Coffee time
Second workshop:	Counselor qualifications Organizational structure of camp Counseling techniques Traditions and policies Preparing for camp Challenges of counseling (conducted before a fireplace if possible) Prayertime
Third workshop:	What to bring to camp Health and safety Characteristics of age-groups Camper needs and goal-setting Program planning Demonstration of an evening program Prayer for campers
Fourth workshop:	Camper guidance Camp morale Camper participation Records and evaluation Demonstration of camp music Snacks
Fifth Workshop (conducted outdoors in a park):	Campcraft skills—fire-laying, tripping, outdoor cooking, use of knife and ax, orienteering and compass Build fires and cook meal together
Sixth workshop:	Use of the Bible: quiet time, Bible study, cabin devotions, campfire message, leading a camper to Christ, the Word of God lived in camp, devotional Bible study together Prayertime

Seventh workshop: Daily schedules
Activity planning for the week
Rainy-day plans
Cabin-time activities
Plan for special programs (and perhaps special days) in camp
Prayer together

Eighth workshop: First aid
Health education in camp
Follow-up
Prayertime

Pre-in-camp training (conducted at camp): Become familiar with site and area
Emergency fire drill
Waterfront instructions (swimming, boating)
Familiarization with riflery, archery, horsemanship, handcraft, and nature programs
Staff gets settled in cabins
Challenge from the director and prayer

A pre-in-camp training weekend could be scheduled something like this:

CAMP TOMAHAWK'S PRE-IN-CAMP TRAINING WEEKEND, JUNE 17-19

Friday

6:00 Supper
7:30 Let's sing!
8:30 Starlight walk
9:15 Snack
10:00 Cabin devotions with unit leaders

Saturday

7:30 One eye open!
8:00 Flag raising
8:10 Quiet time
8:30 Breakfast
9:00 The unique Camp Tomahawk (philosophy, aims)
9:30 Bible discovery (how to get campers to use their Bibles)
10:45 What you give and receive (counselor qualifications; go over job analysis and agreements)
11:30 Cookout
1:30 Music in camp

2:00 "You are there" (counseling techniques, demonstrations by administrative staff)
3:00 Daily schedules, special programming
4:15 Meeting with activity specialists
5:15 Camper problems (role playing)
6:00 Supper
7:00 What makes a good evening program?
7:30 Campfire (demonstration of a good campfire program)
8:30 Snack, discussion
9:00 Get ready for . . .
9:30 Cabin devotions (demonstrations by unit leaders)

Sunday

8:00 The eyes have it!
8:30 Flag raising
8:40 Quiet time
9:00 Breakfast
10:00 The point of decision (leading a camper to Christ)
11:00 Church (challenge to staff by director)
12:30 Dinner
1:30 Farewell till . . .

If all of your staff contacts are just prior to camp, you may conduct a training program like this:

CAMP TREETOP'S PRE-IN-CAMP TRAINING WEEK

Monday

Morning: Check in
Get settled
Get acquainted
Snacks
Group devotions and prayer
Go over training session agenda
Afternoon: General objectives of camping
Philosophy and traditions
Waterfront organization, regulations, swimming tests
Evening: Song-leading techniques
Group singing
Teach good camp songs

Tuesday

Morning: Quiet-time suggestions
Discussions
Program objectives
Principles and procedures for group living

	Program planning for special days
Afternoon:	Canoeing instruction, swimming instruction
	Nature projects and nature trails
Evening:	More camp songs, storytelling methods
	Camp skits
	Demonstration of an evening program
	Star study, from canoes on the lake

Wednesday
(a day in camp)

Morning:	Bible study methods (participation and demonstration)
Afternoon:	Visit activity areas (craft shop, rifle and archery ranges, waterfront)
Evening:	Film on camping
	Role playing
	Evening program

Thursday

Morning:	Bible teaching (principles and practice)
	Campcraft skills (knots and lashing)
Afternoon:	Counseling methods, camper characteristics
	Setting goals, fire-building, cook dinner out
	Plan canoe trip
Evening:	Tripping techniques
	Safety, health, first aid

Friday

Morning:	Cabin devotion planning, campfire messages and programs, research projects
Afternoon:	Leave for canoe trip
Evening:	Setting up camp, cookout, counselors put on evening program and campfire service, overnight

Saturday

Morning:	Return to camp after breakfast
Afternoon:	Clean and return camping gear, evaluate trip
Evening:	Craft program, daily schedules, rainy-day activities

Sunday

Morning:	Bible study, worship service
Afternoon:	Explore surrounding area, rest, relax
Evening:	Vespers on the beach and challenge

Monday

Morning:	Prepare for campers' arrival

Use variety in your training sessions. Some methods and techniques you may use include: talks, discussions, lectures, demonstrations, practice of skills, participation, case studies, summaries, narrative accounts, projects, assignments, observations, slapboard visuals, publications, research, role playing, buzz sessions, brainstorming, panels, group conversations, debates, forums, films, charts, diagrams, overhead projections, exhibits, symposiums, listening teams, group interviews, interest-finders, checklists, and models.

Perhaps you will challenge your staff in a campfire message the night before the campers arrive. Help them realize the *urgency* in the task before them. Help them broaden their vision to see what God wants to do at camp this summer, in the lives of campers and in their own lives.

You may remind your counselors that a Christian camp, partly because of its concentrated impact and its controlled environment, can be effective in winning, training, and sending campers out for Jesus Christ. A truly Christian atmosphere at camp provides a healthy climate for Christian growth, and the personal relationships between each counselor and his campers are important to the campers' spiritual progress. This means that counselors must be dedicated, well-trained, and Spirit-sensitive.

May Christ help you and your staff to practice what you teach, so that many campers will learn to love and obey Him at your camp.

MATERIALS FOR COUNSELORS

	John Johnson	Karla Jones	Evelyn Erickson	Thomas Tillson	Mary Smith	Amy Perkins	
Application sent, received	✓	✓	✓	✓	✓	✓	
Contract sent, received	✓			✓			
Letter 1	✓			✓			
Letter 2				✓			
Letter 3							
Job analysis							
Health form							
Cabin assignment							
Activity helps							
Cabin devotion helps							
Bible study Instructor's Manual and Camper's Do-It Book							
Quiet-time suggestions							
Interview							
Books							
Magazines							
Special helps							
What-to-bring list							
Training session #1							
Training session #2							
Pre-in-camp training							
Thank-you letter							

APPENDIX

SAMPLE CAMP STAFF APPLICATION

(Mr.)
Name(Mrs.) ________________________ Date of application ____________
(Miss)
Address ________________________________ Phone ____________
(Street) (City) (State)

Height ________ Weight ________ Age ________ Sex ________ Race ________

Church affiliation ________________________ Pastor ________________

Major church activities ________________________________

Education: High school ________________________ College ________________

Special training ________________________________

Present occupation ________________________________

In good health? ______ Any physical handicaps? ______ Describe ________________

Experience as camper (years and places) ________________________

____

Camp staff experience (years and places) ________________________

Special camp responsibilities ________________________

Camp position desired (counselor, cook, instructor, nurse, etc.) ________________

With what age group(s) do you work best? ________________________

In the following list, put 1 before activities you can organize and teach; 2 for those in which you can assist in teaching; 3 for those with which you are slightly familiar.

GROUP ACTIVITIES

__ Bible study
__ Missions study
__ Vocational guidance
__ Campfire programs
__ Camp newspaper
__ Storytelling
__ Skits and stunts
__ Treasure hunts and like games
__ ________________

SPORTS

__ Archery
__ Badminton
__ Riding
__ Riflery
__ Softball
__ Table tennis
__ Tennis
__ Track and field
__ Volley ball
__ ________________

NATURE

__ Animals
__ Astronomy
__ Birds
__ Forestry
__ Insects
__ Plants (flowers, trees, shrubs)
__ Rocks and minerals
__ Weather
__ ________________

PIONEERING

__ Camp craft
__ Fishing
__ Hiking
__ Outdoor cooking
__ Overnight camping
__ Map-making

COUNSELING

__ Educational talks
__ Individual counseling
__ ________________

MUSIC

__ Lead singing
Instruments (list)
__ Accordion
__ Bugle
__ Piano
__ ________________

WATERFRONT

__ Aquaplaning
__ Canoeing
__ Diving
__ Lifesaving
__ Rowing
__ Sailing
__ Swimming
__ Water skiing
__ ________________

Swimming classification (check)
__ Advanced
__ Intermediate
__ Beginner
__ Nonswimmer

MISCELLANEOUS

__ Library
__ Nurse
__ Typing
__ ________________

JOB ANALYSIS
Camp Babbling Brook for Girls

Position: Cabin Counselor
Responsible to: Unit Director
Responsibilities:

General—
Care for the needs of the cabin group.
Cooperate with other counselors and staff members.
Perform tasks other than those assigned, if asked.

Specific—
Strive to meet the individual needs of campers.
Conduct Bible study with your cabin group each day.
Conduct cabin devotions with the cabin each night.
Endeavor to lead each unconverted camper to Christ.
Help each Christian camper to have a meaningful quiet time, to learn and live by the truths he finds in God's Word.
Speak at evening campfire.
Make reports as required.
Lead in the following activities:

Assist in these activities:

COUNSELOR AGREEMENT
Camp Sunny Rock

This is to confirm the understanding between Camp Sunny Rock and ______________________________, that he will fill the position of ______________________________ at this camp. He will be expected to be at camp from __________ to __________. He will attend precamp training sessions on ______________ ________________________ (unless excused).

Responsibilities of the Administration to the Counselor:

To undertake the expenses of room, board, and insurance

To provide 2 free hours a day for the counselor's personal use and one 12-hour day a week free

To help the staff member adjust to his responsibilities and to acquaint him with the camp's goals and philosophy

To supervise and help the counselor in any way that seems advisable

To pay a weekly salary of $X.XX. [Editor's note: Many Christian camps do not pay their counselors.]

Responsibility of the Counselor to the Camp:

To be a constructive member of the staff, contributing in every way possible to the camp's health, harmony, and happiness

To be loyal to the aims, policies, and regulations of the camp

To live with the campers as companion and guide and assume some responsibility for their spiritual and physical welfare

To pray for each camper in his care

To seek to lead unconverted campers to the Saviour

To help each Christian camper grow in the Lord, believing and obeying what he reads in God's Word

To be willing to go beyond the call of duty when needed

To prepare for Bible study and activities before camp opens

To be present at all staff meetings

To voice any criticism to the director first
To take part in the camp follow-up program

It is understood that the Administration reserves the right to dismiss any member of the staff, if the best interests of the camp demand it.

This agreement is signed prayerfully, understanding that its fulfillment is to glorify the Lord.

Date ____________ Signature of Counselor ________________
Date __________ Signature of Camp Director ______________

SAMPLE CAMPER EVALUATION

CAMPER EVALUATION
(to be completed by counselor at end of camp)

Dear Pastor____________________: Here's a report on ______________________________.

He (She) attended Camp ______________________________ from ________ to ________, 196___.

This status and progress report should help you better understand and guide him (her). Please pass this form on to his (her) Sunday School teacher. (If the camper doesn't attend Sunday School, we suggest that____.)

Counselor making report ______________________________ Date ____________________

Camper's street address ____

City ______________________________ State ______________ Phone ______________

Age ________ Grade (this fall) ________ Sex ________ Race ________

	YES	NO
Did assigned Bible work		
Reads Bible on his own		
Tells others about the Lord		
Growing in faith		
Athletically inclined		

	YES	NO
Used to being away from home		
Critical, fault-finding		
Easily discouraged		
Tries to domineer		
Sense of inferiority		

Stronger qualities ____

Weaker qualities ____

Main interests ____

Physical disabilities or health problems (if any) ______________________________

____

Skills developed during camp ____

____

Swimming classification: Advanced ☐ Intermediate ☐ Beginner ☐ Nonswimmer ☐

Spiritual decision(s) made at camp (what and when) ______________________________

____

Apparent results of my personal counseling ______________________________

____

My opinion of camper's present spiritual status ______________________________

____

(Any additional comments on back of this sheet.)

PARENT QUESTIONNAIRE

Camp Northwilds

Dear Parents:

This questionnaire has grown out of our desire for the intelligent cooperation of parents who recognize the educational value of camp. You will aid us immeasurably by answering fully and frankly these questions, thereby pointing out ways in which Camp Northwilds may help your boy or girl grow in Christian character and all-around development. It will interest you and us to note changes of attitude during camp and to observe how these changes carry over into school and home situations. (Only those directly responsible for your child will have access to the following information.)

Camper's name ______________ Grade in the fall ________ Age _____

Average grade in school ______________ Height ______ Weight ______

Ages of brother(s) ______________ Ages of sister(s) ______ ________

Church he attends ____

Is attendance regular for the youth? ______ For others in family? ______

What childhood diseases or other illnesses has he had? ____________

____

Does he catch cold easily? _____ Is he troubled with constipation? _____

Has he had any nervous disorders, such as hysteria, fainting spells, seizures? If so, what and when? ________________________________

Will any past or present illnesses or allergies prevent him from taking part in any camp activity? If so, discuss. ______________________________

____

Does he have any special fears? If so, what? ______________________

Are there any foods that he should not eat? ______________________

____

What responsibilities does he have at home? ______________________

Has he a regular allowance? _______ How much per week? _________

What are his hobbies? ____________________________________

What games does he play? _________________________________

What are his stronger qualities? ____________________________

What are his weaker qualities? _____________________________

What would you like him to receive from his camp experience? _______

____

Has he made a profession of salvation?

To what extent is he used to being away from his parents? __________

____

Is he troubled with bed-wetting? ____________________________

Does he usually try to lead or follow? _________________________

What does *he* want to get from his camp experience? (Ask him.) _______

____

Phone ____________ Parents' signatures: ______________________

____

Address: _____ __________________________

Bibliography

Administration

_______. *Camp Standards with Interpretation for the Accreditation of Organized Camps*. Martinsville, Ind.:American Camping Association.

_______. *Foundations for Excellence.* Wheaton, Ill.: Christian Camping International.

Mitchell, Viola and Meier, Joel. *Camp Counseling*. Philadelphia: W.B. Saunders, 1983.

Rodney, Lynn S. and Ford, Phyllis M. *Camp Administration*. New York: John Wiley and Sons, 1970.

Arts and Crafts

Barnes, Charles and Blake, David. *Creative Macrame Projects*. New York: Dover Publications, 1971.

_______. *Basketry* (No. 3313). New Brunswick, N.J.: Boy Scouts of America, 1968.

Benson, Kenneth R. *Creative Crafts for Children*. Englewood Cliffs, N.J.: Prentice-Hall, Inc., 1958.

Cherry, Raymond. *Leathercrafting Procedures and Projects*. Bloomington, Ill.: McKnight Publishing Co., 1979.

Griswold, Lester and Griswold, Kathleen. *The New Handcraft Processes and Projects*. New York: Van Nostrand Co., 1972.

Guptill, Arthur. *Pencil Drawing: Step by Step*. New York: Van Nostrand Co., 1979.

Hunt, W. Ben. *Indian Crafts and Lore.* New York: Western Publishing Co., 1957.

_______. *Leathercraft* (No. 3310). New Brunswick, N.J.: Boy Scouts of America, nd.

Norbeck, Oscar E. *Authentic Indian Life Crafts*. Corvallis, Oreg.: Galloway Publishing Co., 1974.

Zarchy, Harry. *Let's Go Camping*. New York: Alfred A. Knopf Co., 1959.

Bible Study

Edge, Findley B. *Teaching for Results*. Nashville: Broadman Press, 1956.

Jensen, Irving L. *Enjoy Your Bible*. Chicago: Moody Press, 1969.

LeBar, Lois. *Children in the Bible School*. Old Tappan, N.J.: Fleming H. Revell Company, 1952.

Miles, Mary. *Devotions for Pre-teens #3*. Chicago: Moody Press, 1971.

Todd, Floyd and Todd, Pauline. *Good Morning, Lord: Devotions for Campers*. Grand Rapids: Baker Book House, 1974.

Wald, Oletta. *The Joy of Discovery*. Minneapolis: Bible Banner Press, nd.

———. *You Can Help a New Christian*. Schroon Lake, N.Y.: Word of Life, Inc., nd.

Zuck, Roy and Benson, Warren. *Youth Work in the Church*. Chicago: Moody Press, 1978.

Counseling

Adams, Jay. *Competent to Counsel*. Grand Rapids: Baker Book House, 1977.

Camper Guidance—A Basic Handbook for Counselors. Martinsville, Ind.: American Camping Association, nd.

Duvall Evelyn. *Parent and Teenager*. New York: Broadman Press, 1976.

Ensign, John and Ensign, Ruth. *Camping Together as Christians*. Richmond, Va.: John Knox Press, 1958.

Felske, Norma. *You Can Teach Young Teens*. Wheaton, Ill.: Victor Books, 1976.

Mattson, Lloyd, *The Camp Counselor*, Duluth, Minn.: Camping Guideposts, 1983.

Mitchell, Viola and Meier, Joel. *Camp Counseling*. Philadelphia: W.B. Saunders, 1983.

Narramore, Clyde M. *The Psychology of Counseling*. Grand Rapids: Zondervan Publishing House, 1960.

Todd, Floyd and Todd, Pauline. *Camping for Christian Youth*. Grand Rapids: Baker Book House, 1968.

Understanding Campers

Bloom, Joel W. et al. *Camper Guidance—A Basic Handbook for Counselors*. Martinsville, Ind.: American Camping Association, 1961.

Budd, William C. *Behavior Modification*. Plainfield, N.J.: Galloway Publications, 1973.

Hartwig, Marie and Myers, Betty. *Camping Leadership—Counseling and Programming*. Minneapolis: Burgess Publishing Co., 1976.

McDaniel, Elsiebeth. *You Can Teach Primaries*. Wheaton, Ill.: Victor Books, 1976.

Mitchell, Viola and Meier, Joel. *Camp Counseling*. Philadelphia: W.B. Saunders Co., 1983.

Musselman, Virginia. *The Day Camp Program Book*. New York: Association Press, 1963.

Shivers, Jay S. *Camping: Administration, Counseling, Programming*. Englewood Cliffs, N.J.: Prentice-Hall, Inc., 1971.

Smith, Julian. *Outdoor Education*. Englewood Cliffs, N.J.: Prentice-Hall, Inc., 1972.

Wright, Norman. *Help, I'm a Counselor*. Glendale, Calif.: Regal Books, 1968.

Program

American Red Cross books on: *Basic Canoeing, Basic Rowing, Basic Sailing, Swimming and Diving, Lifesaving, First Aid* and *Emergency Care*.

Angier, Bradford. *Home in Your Pack*. New York: The Macmillan Co., 1972.

_______. *How To Stay Alive in the Woods*. New York: The Macmillan Co., 1962.

_______. *Survival with Style*. Harrisburg, Pa.: Stackpole Books, 1972.

Bridge, Raymond. *America's Backpacking Book*. New York: Charles Scribner's Sons, 1973.

Brown, Vinson. *Reading the Woods*. New York: The Macmillan Co., 1969.

_______. *Field Book*. New Brunswick, N.J.: Boy Scouts of America, nd.

Graendorf, Werner and Mattson, Lloyd. *An Introduction to Christian Camping*. Chicago: Moody Press, 1979.

Kephart, Horace. *Camping and Woodcraft*. New York: The Macmillan Company, 1948.

_______. *Knots and How to Tie Them*. New Brunswick, N.J.: Boy Scouts of America, nd.

Lanoue, Fred. *Drownproofing*. Englewood Cliffs, N.J.: Prentice-Hall, Inc., 1963.

Mackay, Joy. *Raindrops Keep Falling on My Tent*. Martinsville, Ind.: American Camping Association, 1982.

Meier, Joel F. *Backpacking*. Dubuque, Iowa: William C. Brown and Co., 1980.

Merrill, W.K. *The Survival Handbook*. New York: Winchester Press, 1972.

Rethmel, R.C. *Backpacking*. Martinsville, Ind.: American Camping Association, 1965.

Rohnke, Karl. *Cowtails and Cobras*. Hamilton, Mass.: Project Adventure, 1977.

———. *Weather*. New Brunswick, N.J.: Boy Scouts of America, 1963.

Nature and Conservation

Adams, George F. and Wyckoff, Jerome. *Landforms: A Guide to Rock Scenery*. New York: Western Publishing Company, Inc., 1971.

Alexander, Taylor R. and Fichter, George S. *Ecology*. New York: Western Publishing Company, Inc., 1973.

Burt, William H. *Field Guide to the Birds*, rev. ed. Boston: Houghton Mifflin Company, 1947.

Carr, Marion B. *Oceanography*. New York: Western Publishing Company, Inc., 1973.

Carson, Rachel. *Silent Spring*. New York: Fawcett World Publishing Company, 1973.

Conant, Roger. *Field Guide to Reptiles and Amphibians*. Roger T. Peterson, ed. Boston: Houghton Mifflin Company, 1958.

Gaudette, Marie. *Leader's Nature Guide*. New York: Girl Scouts of America, 1942.

Hillcourt, William. *Field Book of Nature Activities and Hobbies*. New York: G.P. Putnam's Sons, 1961.

Klots, Alexander B. *Field Guide to the Butterflies*. Roger T. Peterson, ed. Boston: Houghton Mifflin Company, 1951.

Levi, Herbert W. and Levi, Lorna R. *Spiders and Their Kin*. New York: Western Publishing Company, Inc., 1969.

Menzel, Donald H. *Field Guide to the Stars and Planets*. Roger T. Peterson, ed. Boston: Houghton Mifflin Company, 1964.

Mitchell, Robert and Zim, Herbert S. *Butterflies and Moths*. New York: Western Publishing Company, Inc., 1964.

Morris, Percy A. *Field Guide to Atlantic Coast Shells,* 3rd ed. Boston: Houghton Mifflin Company, 1973.

———. *Field Guide to Pacific Coast Shells.* Boston: Houghton Mifflin Company, 1964.

Murie, Olans. *Field Guide to Animal Tracks*, 2nd ed. Roger T. Peterson, ed. Boston: Houghton Mifflin Company, 1975.

Nickelsburg, Janet. *Ecology, Habitats, Niches, and Food Chains*. New York: J.B. Lippincott Company, 1969.

Ormond, Clyde. *Complete Book of Outdoor Lore*. New York: Harper and Row Publishers, Inc., 1982.

Peterson, Roger T. *Field Guide to the Birds,* rev. ed. Boston: Houghton Mifflin Company, 1947.

Peterson, Roger T. and MacKenney, Margaret. *Field Guide to Wildflowers of Northeastern and Central North America*. Boston: Houghton Mifflin Company, 1968.

Petrides, George A. *Field Guide to Trees and Shrubs*. Boston: Houghton Mifflin Company, 1973.

Reid, George K. *Pond Life*. Herbert S. Zim, ed. New York: Western Publishing Company, Inc., 1967.

Rhodes, Frank H. *Geology*. New York: Western Publishing Company, Inc. 1971.

Shuttleworth, Floyd S. and Zim, Herbert S. *Non-Flowering Plants*. New York: Western Publishing Company, Inc., 1967.

Van Metre, Steve. *Acclimatizing*. Martinsville, Ind.: American Camping Association, 1974.

Van de Smissen, Betty and Goering, Oswald. *A Leader's Guide to Nature Oriented Activities*. Ames, Iowa: Iowa State University Press, 1977.

Zim, Herbert S. and Baker, Robert H. *Stars*. New York: Western Publishing Company, Inc., 1951.

Zim, Herbert S. and Cottam, Clarence A. *Insects*. New York: Western Publishing Company, Inc. 1951.

Zim, Herbert S. and Gabrielson, Ira N. *Birds*. New York: Western Publishing Company, Inc., 1949.

Zim, Herbert S. and Hoffmeister, Donald F. *Mammals*. New York: Western Publishing Company, Inc. 1955.

Zim, Herbert S. and Martin, Alexander C. *Flowers*. New York: Western Publishing Company, Inc. 1950.

———. *Trees*. New York: Western Publishing Company, Inc., 1952.

Games and Recreation

Buskin, David. *Outdoor Games*. New York: Sayre Publishing Company, 1966.

Eisenburg, Larry and Eisenberg, Helen. *Fun and Fellowship Resource Book*. Grand Rapids: Baker Book House, 1981.

_______. *Handy Games*. Delaware, Ohio: Cooperative Recreation, nd.

Harbin, E.O. *Old Fashion Games and Fun*. Grand Rapids: Baker Book House, 1978.

Mackay, Joy. *Raindrops Keep Falling on My Tent*. Martinsville, Ind.: American Camping Association, 1982.

Mulac, Margaret E. *Fun and Games*. New York: The Macmillan Company, 1963.

Richardson, Hazel A. *Games for the Elementary School Grades*. Minneapolis: Burgess Publishing Company, 1951.

Tripping

Bearse, Ray. *The Canoe Camper's Handbook*. New York: Winchester Press, 1974.

Bridge, Raymond. *America's Backpacking Book*. New York: Charles Scribner's Sons, 1973.

Gibbons, Euell. *Stalking the Wild Asparagus*. New York: David McKay Co., Inc., 1970.

Meier, Joel. *Backpacking*. Dubuque, Iowa: William C. Brown and Co., 1980.

Thomas, Dian. *Roughing It Easy*. Provo, Utah: Brigham Young University Press, 1976.

Wilderness Pocket N' Pack Library—*Survival in the Wilderness, Poisonous Plants in the Wilderness, Edible Plants in the Wilderness*. Manning, Oreg.: Life Support Technology, nd.

Helpful Organizations

American Camping Association, Bradford Woods, Martinsville, Ind. 46151

American Orienteering Society, 220 Fiftieth Avenue, New York, N.Y. 10001

American National Red Cross, 17th and D Streets, Washington, D.C. 20006

Archery Institute, 715 North Rush Street, Chicago, Ill. 60611

Camp Archery Association, 200 Coligni Avenue, New Rochelle, N.J. 10801

Christian Camping International, Box 646, Wheaton, Ill. 60189

Cooperative Recreation Service, Radnor Road, Delaware, Ohio 43015

National Audubon Society, 1130 Fifth Avenue, New York, N.Y. 10028

National Park Service, 1100 Ohio Drive, S.W., Washington D.C. 20242

National Recreation and Park Association, 1700 Pennsylvania Avenue, Washington, D.C. 20006

National Rifle Association, 1600 Rhode Island Avenue, N.W., Washington D.C. 20036

The Outdoor Education Association, Inc., 606 South Marion, Carbondale, Ill. 62901

U.S. Geological Survey, Department of the Interior, Washington, D.C. 20244

Windsurfing International Inc., 3065 Rt. 6 and 28, Cranberry Highway, East Wareham, Mass. 02538